You're Never Too Young

Also Available in Large Print
by Lawrence Welk with Bernice McGeehan:

This I Believe

You're Never Too Young

by

Lawrence Welk

with

Bernice McGeehan

G.K.HALL &CO.
Boston, Massachusetts
1982

Library of Congress Cataloging in Publication Data

Welk, Lawrence, 1903-
    You're never too young.

    1. Welk, Lawrence, 1903-   . 2. Conductors (Music)
--United States--Biography. I. McGeehan, Bernice.
II. Title.
ML422.W33A33 1982   785.4'1'0924   [B]   82-3092
ISBN 0-8161-3390-5   AACR2

Published in Large Print by arrangement with Prentice-Hall, Inc.

Set in 18 pt English Times

Contents

1. Matty

I've had a lot in my life to be grateful for. But I doubt if anything will surpass a November afternoon in 1980 when I sat in a darkened movie theater, surrounded by some of those I love best in this world, and watched the story of my life unfold before my eyes. There, on the huge cinemascope screen in front of me, were pictures from my past—my mother, my father, the farm where I grew up, the church where we worshiped—even a picture of me with my first accordion. Was that skinny, awkward, bashful young fellow up there on the screen really me? I watched as the story moved along, and my eyes began to fill with tears as I saw some of the people who were so important in my life—George T. Kelly, in a scene taken from the old television show *This Is Your Life,* in which both of us

1

broke into tears; photographs of my little five-piece band in the twenties; pictures of my matchless Fern, without whom my life could never have been successful; snapshots of our children and our home in River Forest, Illinois; scenes from our early television shows with some of the artists who became friends with America—the little Lennon Sisters, Pete Fountain, Aladdin, Dick Kesner; more scenes of our stars of today—all so gifted, so talented, so dear to my heart.

As the movie ended in a surge of beautiful music, the house lights came up and our son, Larry, hopped on stage, microphone in hand, to introduce those who had produced the film. Smiling, he motioned me to join him. But I just couldn't. My eyes were too red from weeping, and even Fern was close to tears. "But I don't dare cry," she whispered to me under cover of the tumultuous applause. "If I do, my contact lens will fall out!" I gripped her hand tightly as the audience continued to cheer and applaud, and I don't know when I've felt more proud, more fulfilled and happy. There on stage was our son, who had helped organize and arrange this entire project. Around us in the theater were so many of those who mean so much to us—George Cates, who had directed the music for the film; Jim Hobson, who had first envisioned it; Bob Warren, who had narrated it; Bernice McGeehan, who had written it; Ted Lennon, the mastermind behind the whole project; and seated around us in the audience so many of my "kids" from the band, everyone from Barney Liddell and Myron Floren to the little Aldridge sisters and the Otwell twins. As I looked around that sea of smiling, loving faces, I realized as never before how important people are in your life. No one makes a success of his life alone. I have been helped and inspired and boosted along by wonderful people all my life; my success is their success, is *our* success. John Donne said, "No man is an island." He said it much more poetically than I, but I understand what he meant, especially as I grow older.

To a large extent it is our relationships with other people which determine our success in life, and there are so many for whom I feel great gratitude and affection. I've mentioned in some of my other books how I feel about George T. Kelly who gave me my start; about Eddie Weisfeldt, who got me "talking"; about Tom Archer, who helped me learn the ballroom business; Don Fedderson and Sam Lutz, who have been with me through all the television years; Lois Lamont and her sister Laurie Rector who have been my loyal and superlative secretaries ever since I can remember; and—about Matty Rosenhaus.

I don't want to start this book on a sad note, but I do want to share with you the tremendous impact this man had on my life and the lives of everyone in our Musical Family. Matty was going to honor us with a foreword to this book. Now he cannot. We lost him in August of 1980. My life will never be the same again.

I cannot forget that day. We had just returned from a two-week stand in Las Vegas and were at the studio taping a show when the phone rang about eleven in the morning. I could hear Laurie talking, and then she came into my inner dressing room and said, "Sam is going to call you in a minute, Lawrence. Why don't you just sit here on the sofa and be comfortable?"

I did as she suggested, thinking I would tease Sam about some minor surgery he had just undergone, and when the phone rang I picked it up and caroled, "Hellooo,

Sammy-boy! How are you?"

But what he had to tell me broke my heart. "Lawrence," he said, "I have sad news. Very sad news. We lost Matty last night. In New York. He had a heart attack."

"Oh, no no no, Sam, don't tell me that," I cried brokenly, "please don't tell me that!"

But of course it was true, and it was probably the severest blow of my life. Matty had been more than my dearest friend, more than a sponsor, more than a man I respected as well as liked. Matty had given me the greatest gift any of us can give another—he believed in me.

He was our sponsor for twenty years. When ABC let us go in 1971, and I was plunged into despair at the thought that my two-hundred-member "family" would be out of a job, Matty was the first to phone and say, "Don't worry, Lawrence. Whatever you decide to do, we'll go along with you. Lawrence—I believe in you." When he said those words, I could no longer hold back tears, but they were tears of joy and gratitude that this fine man had given my boys and girls a new lease on life.

I was aware, all during those years, that

other agents, other artists were continually after Matty, who was chairman of the board of the J. B. Williams Company, to sponsor them. But Matty stayed loyal to us. That kind of loyalty is so rare in the heartless and sometimes cruel world of show business, I cannot even think of any other such relationship on television.

As he believed in and inspired me, so I believed in and tried to inspire the members of our band. As he demonstrated a consistent pattern of love and compassion and understanding, so I tried to emulate him. He was larger than life to all of us who knew him, and in spite of the fact that he was one of the most powerful and successful men in the history of American business, he was a living testament to the power of goodness in human nature. He was never too busy to say a kind word or do a good deed. He was an exemplary husband and father, as his beautiful Gila and their three little girls can testify. And I am not alone in my assessment of him. On the day he died, there was a constant procession of people to my dressing room, their eyes swollen from weeping, their voices hoarse with emotion, all expressing their shock and grief.

6

I don't know how I got through that day. I cried for three hours straight, and then somehow got hold of myself. Today I believe Matty's strength became my strength. The goodness he lived and radiated reached us even after his death, and enabled us to carry on. Ed Kletter, his associate who has been so close to us all these years, shared our grief as we consoled each other through those black hours. But I was aware, even in the depths of my sorrow, that something was pressing on my mind, some thought was trying to get through, something that would help me accept the enormity of our loss. It was my daughter Donna who finally put it into words. "Dad," she said softly, "maybe this tremendous grief we feel is the price we pay for knowing anyone as wonderful as Matty."

He was as much, or more, a part of our Musical Family as anyone in it, and made it possible for us to bring our kind of entertainment to you fans and friends through all these years. In that sense, he was your friend and patron, too. So it is with a profound sense of gratitude and affection that I dedicate this book to the memory of Matty.

2. Never in My Wildest Dreams!

Never in my wildest dreams did I ever think I would become an actor! In fact if you've read some of my earlier books, you may recall how a showman named George T. Kelly tried to make an actor out of me way back in the twenties. After a few frustrating months, he gave up completely and solved the problem by casting me as the corpse in the murder-mystery plays we presented. Forty years later, Jack Benny and Lucille Ball tried to make an actor out of me, too. I guess I hadn't improved much—the first time I rehearsed with Lucille, she watched me for about two minutes and then rushed over to a friend of mine, crying, "Are you his dramatic coach? Well, for heaven's sake, *help* him!"

The Good Lord and every one else knows I'm no actor and never was, and that's why

I was so surprised to find myself, one fine spring day last year, "acting" in front of a camera, a movie director, and a whole crowd of interested onlookers. I was even more surprised to find my wife, Fern, acting right alongside me. I was not only surprised, I was flabbergasted, because Fern makes exactly one TV appearance per year —on our Christmas show—and then I have to beg and plead a little. But for this movie she not only agreed, she insisted! "Well," as she said logically enough when I asked her about it, "I'm not an entertainer, so there's no reason for me to appear on your television show. But this movie you're making is the story of your life—so I *should* be in it."

Right. But I still didn't know how—or who—had talked her into it, and I watched, amazed, as she joined in enthusiastically on all the plans. She had long conferences with Rose Weiss, our costume designer, about what to wear, and I must confess when she walked out on the movie sound stage wearing a pale pink chiffon waltz gown and a double strand of pearls, she looked so pretty I could hardly wait to show her off. Our big scene together was one in which we dance to the strains of "The Anniversary

Waltz." We hadn't had much chance to rehearse, so I kept whispering instructions to her as we swirled and dipped around the small dance floor. "Now I'm going to twirl you under my arm," I hissed through a fixed smile. "Okay," she hissed back. "And when we finish, take a little bow," I added. "Okay," she gritted. What we didn't know was that our body mikes were on, and the crew was listening with interest to every word we said! At the end, Fern made such an endearing little bow I couldn't resist sweeping her into my arms and giving her a big kiss. For a non-professional, she had done a wonderful job, and was just as cool as could be.

But not me! I was scared to death about the whole thing, because "talking" is just not my cup of tea. I don't mind talking to live audiences—in fact, I love it. And I don't mind reading a couple of sentences off cue cards for our television show. But in this case I had to narrate a whole half-hour movie and perform in front of the camera all by myself.

Perhaps I had better backtrack here and explain why we were making a movie in the first place. As some of you may know, we have a mobile-home resort near Escondido,

10

California, about forty miles north of San Diego. No one was more surprised than I when it turned out to be a resort. . . . I certainly didn't plan it that way. When Ted Lennon and Bert Carter (the man who was initially responsible for Dodge Motor Company sponsoring us on television) drove me down into the southern California area back in 1964 to look for possible investments, I was mainly looking for a way to take advantage of the magnificent climate and find a vacation retreat, a home away from home for Fern and myself, possibly an avocado ranch or something of that sort. But the minute I set eyes on a lovely little nine-hole golf course built around a small mobile-home park, covered with spreading oak trees, I just fell in love with the place. I went to work enlarging the course to eighteen holes as soon as I acquired it, and adding a small restaurant and a few motel rooms, but visitors began to come in such numbers we were soon obliged to add another motel unit and enlarge the restaurant. And still they came, in such increasing numbers that we added two more large motel units, a couple more swimming pools and Jacuzzis, some banquet facilities, a clubhouse to serve the expanding mobile-home section and finally, three night-lighted tennis courts—and one day I woke up to the fact that we had ourselves quite a resort. But one thing bothered me. I couldn't always be there to greet our guests, and I wanted to do something extra for them while they were there—something to say thank you for all the love and support they have given our television show.

It was along about that time that somebody suggested adding a theater and a museum. "We could make a movie of your life to show in the theater—and collect old photographs and band memorabilia to display in a museum. That should be interesting for the guests." I wish I could tell you who was the first to come up with this idea. Jim Hobson, our incomparable producer-director, was no doubt the first, but our musical director, George Cates, and executive vice-president, Ted Lennon, and several others had much the same idea, and I myself had been thinking along those lines for several years. At any rate, we all agreed the idea had potential, and when we were planning to add a couple hundred new mobile-home spaces in our Village in 1978, it seemed like an ideal time to build a

graphic designer, Luann Rockman, were very young, but they seemed to grasp the "homey," warm feeling we wanted, and I felt very lucky to have found them.

With the plans for the movie under way, we began turning our attention to ideas and concepts for the museum, and the entire project began to assume such major proportions that Ted asked my son, Larry, to step in and oversee it. I was delighted when he agreed. Larry has been president of Ranwood Records for many years, and I knew from experience what a great organizer he is. He jumped into action immediately, enlisting George Cates to do the music, Bob Warren to help narrate the script, and Chuck Koon, our wonderful set director on the show, to build the sets for the museum. At that point I relaxed completely and just turned the entire operation over to them. I'm the first to admit that the technical side of the entertainment business is not for me. With me it's music, music, music, and for anything else I just trust the people around me. Sometimes I have no idea what they're doing, but I trust them enough to go along with it.

So *that's* how I found myself, one bright

morning in May, all dressed up in my champagne suit and best dancing shoes, ready to "act" in the movie. Cam and Greg and their crew had come in a couple of days ahead of time and transformed the banquet hall of our restaurant in Escondido into a real movie studio—we had all felt that filming in Escondido itself would help us get the feel we wanted. They had hung heavy black velvet drapes over the walls and windows to help soundproof the room, installed giant lights in a ceiling grid, tracks on the floor for the heavy movie camera to move on, and added complete sound and recording equipment. They had also set up a hundred or so chairs for visitors to watch us work. That helped a great deal, as I found out later on. Unlike television filming, each scene in a movie has to be lighted and set up for the cameraman, and sometimes the wait between scenes is pretty long. For someone like myself, used to the speed of TV, those long waits can be pretty frustrating, and it was a great relief, not to say pleasure, to chat with the audience.

I was really nervous when we began rehearsing and shooting, but as the day wore on, my nervousness wore off, and I began to enjoy it. In the first scene I came

16

out on stage and visited with the folks just as we had planned, and played an old-fashioned pump organ something like the one we had on our farm back home in Strasburg, North Dakota. Joey Schmidt, the young accordion player on our show, had found it for us in Escondido, and it was really fancy, with a mirror on top and needlepoint covers on the foot pedals. In the second scene I played an old German waltz on my accordion, and in the third I spoke of my parents and how they had come to this country in search of freedom. When I described how kind and good and loving they were to us children, I couldn't help getting a lump in my throat, and when I finished, the audience broke into warm, sustained applause. I want to tell you that was the best medicine they could have given me! From then on, things got much easier, and by the time I got to the scene where I confess how I finally agreed to "talk" in public, I was so relaxed I perched on a stool and just sailed through my lines. (For those of you who haven't heard the story, it happened back in the forties when Eddie Weisfeldt, owner of the Riverside Theater in Milwaukee, offered me a booking if I would talk on stage. "I'd like to, Mr.

17

Weisfeldt," I said miserably, "but just listen to me—I *can't* talk!" "Certainly you can," he said, "and it makes no sense for you to sit in the back row of your own band! You should be out in front, emceeing the show." "I'm sorry," I said, "I just can't do it." He shrugged and headed for the door, but with his hand on the knob he suddenly turned and said, "I'll pay you seventeen hundred and fifty dollars a week if you'll talk." "What did you say?" I breathed. His eyes twinkled. "You heard me." "Mr. Weisfeldt," I said, "for that amount of money—I'll talk!" And I've been talking ever since.)

The second day of filming was a repeat of the first, only better. We refilmed some of the scenes we had rehearsed the day before, including my dance with Fern. If the audience had liked her before, they absolutely loved her this time! She made such a hit I complained. "You folks better stop applauding her," I cautioned, "or the stage bug will bite her!" Fern laughed. Being an entertainer is the last thing that would occur to her. She's a nurse, and it's the medical profession that really excites her. Even so, I think she got a real kick out

Strong came up to my office to see me. He was, as Ted had said, a young fellow about twenty-six years old, with a shock of tightly curled blond hair and an open, friendly smile. I liked him right away, but the minute he opened his mouth, we were in deep trouble. At least I was in trouble, because I couldn't understand a word he said in his strong Australian accent. I suppose he had just as much trouble with mine, but we managed to struggle through a little polite conversation, and then Brett got down to business.

First, he got out his calipers and began measuring every inch of my face—my nose, my eyes, my ears, my chin. Then he began taking pictures of me from the top of my head down to my toes, circling me with the camera and click, click, clicking away. "Now smile, Mr. Welk, just like you do in front of the band," he cried. I tried, but it wasn't till I said, "Are you ready, boys?" and counted "Ah-one and ah-two," that I really got in the mood.

That was all the first day. Next day, Brett asked if he could do what he called a life cast of my face. "Sure," I said, never dreaming what was in store for me. I soon found out! He had me lie down flat on the floor of my office, and then smeared some kind of thick goop all over my face and neck. "Now close your eyes," he ordered, "and keep your mouth shut." That was very hard for me—especially the last part, because I like to talk, but I did as he said while he smeared the rest of the goop over my face and ears. "Now," he said sternly, *"don't move!"* After what seemed like an hour, I grunted a little, questioningly. *"No!"* cried Brett, alarmed, "don't talk. It's just a few minutes more." I lay there, wondering how in the world I had let myself get talked into this mess. I had been pushing Ted and Larry to take over more and more responsibility in the organization, true. But now I felt they had gone a little too far. I lay as quietly as I could, and from time to time Brett would pat my cheek. Finally, after about a half hour, he decided I was done. Very, very carefully and gingerly he pried the mask loose from my face and lifted it off. What a relief! It was almost worth doing just to get it off again.

Brett thanked me for my patience and went home to get started. Half an hour later he called. "I'm sorry, Mr. Welk," he said apologetically, "but the mask broke. We'll have to do another one."

Next day we went through the whole routine again . . . lie down, lie quiet, don't move a muscle while the goop is being spread on your face, and *don't talk!* I forgot to tell you that Brett inserted two straws in my nose so I could breathe—I probably looked like a beached walrus. But I didn't care, I was just anxious to get the thing over with. Finally the mask dried and Brett took it off very carefully, went back to his studio to go to work—and discovered that the life cast was of no help at all! "When you lie down," he reported, "all the muscles of your face relax and look very different from the way you look standing up. I'm sorry . . . but the plaster cast is no help. I guess it was just a learning experience for me," he added. (And for me, too, Brett. I learned I didn't want to hold still for another statue!)

By July, Bernice was working very hard every day on the film project, and it seemed that whenever I had a few moments to spare so we could work on this book, she was either in Long Beach working with the Killingsworths or in Escondido working on the museum. I began to despair of ever getting the book done. "Oh, don't worry," she reassured me, "I'm finding out so much about you and the Welk family, researching for the museum, I have enough material for *ten* books!" The way she said it worried me. Every family has a horse thief or two hanging from the family tree, and I was a little afraid of what she might find. I needn't have. The most exciting thing she found, apparently, was the original photograph of my paternal grandparents. "Their names are Johannes (John) and Marianna (Mary) Welk," she informed me excitedly. "Your cousin, Father Tom Welk, sent it to me from Kansas Newman College in Wichita—it was taken in Odessa, Russia, around 1870. Wait till you see it!"

I had never seen a picture of any kind of my grandparents, and I didn't see this one till I got to the museum. There, sure enough, was a photograph of my grandfather sitting stiffly in a chair with my little grandmother standing beside him, her hand on his shoulder—no Women's Liberation in those days, I guess. It was a strange feeling to look into the faces of my grandparents for the first time when I myself was already seventy-seven years of age.

All during the summer months Bernice wrote letters and made follow-up phone calls tracking down information and memorabilia for the museum. My daughter Shirley helped by contributing information she had gleaned from her own research into our family tree, and so did my three sisters back home in Strasburg. In addition, Bernice spent hours on her knees in the basement storeroom of our building, poring through trunks full of old photographs, records, plaques, certificates, contracts, and letters—including one written in 1929, in which I advised a ballroom owner that if the snow was too heavy and prevented people from coming to the ballroom the night he had us booked, I would make it up to him some other date. I had kind of forgotten the weather we used to work in till I read that. I don't recall that it ever really stopped us except for one night when it was so cold only two couples showed up for a dance. After about fifteen freezing minutes, I gave them their money back and we all went home—I figured the two dollars they had paid wouldn't have covered the cost of keeping the place warm anyway.

From time to time Bernice would surface from the depths of the basement to show me one or another of the treasures she had unearthed, and one day she hit the jackpot.

She and Margaret Heron, one of my fabulous secretaries, found nine very old scrapbooks covering the years from the twenties through the fifties, most of which had been lovingly put together by my baby sister, Eva. I was completely lost in memories as I leafed through those fragile, yellowing, brittle pages, particularly when I came across a newspaper clipping head-lined, "Accordion Squeezer Succeeds." It was a column written by music critic Si Steinhauser of Pittsburgh just after we opened at the William Penn Hotel on New Year's Eve in 1938, and I have always felt that his kind review was the one that really launched us on our way.

By October, "Project Escondido" began moving into high gear, and Larry was beginning to look a little frazzled from his constant runs down to Escondido and back. When he came down to the studio one Tuesday, George Cates laughed and said, "Larry, you're starting to look like all the rest of us—worn out!" George himself, with the help of Bob Ballard and Jack Pleis, had managed to do all the arrangements and scoring for the movie, in addition to doing our show every week, and somehow he didn't look too frazzled, but I guess he's used to it. We had decided on November 20th as the day to premiere the movie and dedicate our theater-museum. My staff was urging me to make a big glossy public-relations day out of it and invite a lot of famous guest stars—for a while it sounded as if they were planning to ask the President himself to unveil my statue. But this time I really did put my foot down. "No," I said firmly. "This is a family celebration. If it weren't for the orchestra and the fans, there wouldn't be any theater to dedicate! I want this to be a close, warm family celebration, and just invite our Musical Family and closest friends."

So that's what we did, and, because Escondido is about a hundred miles from Los Angeles, we also decided to arrange round-trip transportation for our guests. "We can hire luxury buses," Larry informed us, "the kind with big seats and a bar and rest rooms." That was news to me—we never had anything like that in the old band-bus days! "And we can serve refreshments en route—soft drinks, sand-wiches, cookies, mints, chocolate brownies." He stopped, frowning. "We'll need hostesses on board to serve . . ."

27

Suddenly, his face cleared. "You folks don't have to worry about that," he announced generously. "I will personally take care of finding hostesses for the bus myself!" As it turned out, the girls in the office agreed to do the job, and on the big day one bus left from our office in Santa Monica at eleven in the morning, and two more from the parking lot of the First Presbyterian Church in Hollywood, which is closer to the San Fernando Valley, where so many of our members live.

But I'm getting ahead of my story. Before that Big Day arrived, there were a few other things to be accomplished—such as a movie to be scored, edited, and put on film; a museum to be decorated; a souvenir book to be written and published; invitations to be addressed and mailed (Margaret Heron volunteered to take over that whole task, and as usual did a superb job) and—unbeknownst to me—a limited edition of numbered bronze commemorative medallions to be struck in honor of the occasion. The last few weeks became a tightly woven sequence of deadlines met just in time to meet new deadlines, and for a while it seemed as if there was one crisis after another. For example, the medallions didn't arrive till two days before the dedication, which meant Larry and his business associate, Chris Hamilton, and their office staff spent one afternoon unwrapping seven hundred bronze medallions from individual, tightly sealed plastic envelopes, rewrapping each one in tissue paper, and then repacking them in brown velvet gift boxes for each guest. They made it just in time.

Two days before the opening, Brett hauled my statue down to set it into place and check to make sure the fountain he had designed was in good working order. I had forgotten about the statue in all the excitement and hadn't had a chance to see it, but Larry and Ted assured me it looked just like me. "That's what I was afraid of," I told them.

Just before the opening, Chuck Koon and his magnificent crew made one last run down to Escondido, inspecting the sets that he'd built, steaming the spectacular pink velvet curtain that hangs from a curved track at the entrance to the museum proper, and making sure all the props and lights were in place and functioning properly. Chuck and his men had done a superb job carrying out Greg Killingsworth's overall concept and design, but somehow I felt that Jim Hobson's brilliance was filtering through, too.

I thought the museum was wonderful when I saw it, and I hope you folks can see it, too, someday. It's really something. Fern and I saw it for the first time the evening before the opening. We had driven down a day early—I really wanted to go on the bus with the rest of the kids, but felt that might make too long and hard a day for me. So we arrived late the evening before, to find Cam and Greg and their associate, Billy Beadle, and Bernice putting up the last of the pictures. It wasn't till about eight o'clock that Fern and I got a chance to see it. It was dark by then, of course, and when Larry threw open the doors I was momentarily blinded, because the first thing you see is the giant crystal champagne glass shown on our TV show every week. It's about ten feet high, and looks even bigger on top of a four-foot-high platform. The champagne glass is really a fountain, and Larry had arranged for it to be turned on. And there it was in all its glory, sending delicate showers of water tinkling into the air, while the thousands and thousands of cut-crystal drops sparkled in a thousand different colors under the spotlights glowing and glimmering like a giant star. I was just dazzled.

The whole room was dramatically lighted, melting into shadows, and had that air of quiet readiness a darkened theater has just before the moment of opening. It held somewhat the same kind of thrill, and I must confess that as Fern and I walked from one exhibit to another, I was deeply touched. It was just like walking through my own life, from the farm in Strasburg to the TV set of today. I shook my head with disbelief when I saw the farm set. It looked so real! Against the wall was an old pump organ just like the one I learned to play when I was about three years old; on the table were a kerosene lamp and an old family Bible; and at the window potted red geraniums and lace curtains, just as my mother used to have.

Next to it was the WNAX set, a replica of the radio station where my little band and I made our debut in Yankton, South Dakota, so many years ago. And next to it was a ballroom stage, with a movie screen running a continuous display of a short the boys and I made back in the forties or fifties—I forget which, but it was when we had a lady trumpet player in the band. Fern and I stood entranced, looking and listening, and all I can say is, George Cates has certainly made a big improvement!

At one end of the room was a giant photographic display which covered all the years of our musical history, and at the other a picture that made everybody gasp. It was huge—and when I say huge, I mean huge, from floor to ceiling and perhaps fourteen feet wide. It's a close-up of me holding a baby girl, with both of us beaming from ear to ear—my teeth look like they're three feet high! I'll let you in on a little secret. That particular baby girl is a real favorite of mine, because her parents are, too—Guy and Ralna. The picture caught little Julie and me at a very happy time, during a Christmas show when I was tossing her into the air.

When I finished my tour that evening, I could see that the little group who had worked so hard to put the museum together was watching me anxiously for my reaction. "Kids," I said, sweeping them all into a bear hug, "I love it. I think you've done a wonderful job. And I just can't wait to see the movie tomorrow. I know it's going to be great."

It was. It was just wonderful, but then so was the whole day. I had gone to bed early so I would be well rested for the next day's activities, and I was up very early as usual and down in the restaurant having breakfast by seven o'clock. Then—ham that I am—I couldn't resist getting out my accordion and playing for the folks. The ceremonies were set to start at one-thirty, and when Ted came in at noon and found me still playing, he cried, "What are you doing here? You're supposed to be taking a nap!"

I took the hint and drove back up the hill to our hilltop home. But instead of taking a nap, I got dressed and stalled around till one-fifteen, when Fern and I drove back down the hill to wait for the incoming buses. And when those three big buses rolled up, and all my Musical Children got out, looking somehow different in these surroundings but just as dear and familiar as ever, I knew it was going to be one of "those" days—and I better keep a hankie handy.

I just wish you folks could have been there. The party started out on the patio, which lies between the theater-museum and the shopping center. It had been freshly planted with trees and flowers, and there were brass musical instruments and musical notes (which Brett had created) embedded in all the walkways of the courtyard. My statue was still shrouded under what looked like a tent, but Brett's fountain was working fine, sending up streams of water into the air, against the blue, blue, blue sky. Colored pennants fluttered in the warm breeze, and there was a long refreshment table covered with giant bowls of punch, cookies, sandwiches, hors d'oeuvres, and a nonstop supply of champagne. We all milled around, exchanging hugs and kisses, admiring the outside of the theater, which sported a big billboard announcing the "World Premiere" of our movie, and enjoying the heady excitement of the day. But even in the midst of all the clamor, Margaret Heron stuck to her job, checking off each arrival and handing each guest a name tag. "Wear this," she commanded. "No name tag—no dinner!"

Suddenly a helicopter appeared overhead, its rotors stirring up such a breeze and making such a racket that conversation was impossible. I gazed upward in astonishment. What in the world was a helicopter doing hovering right over our heads? It stayed so long I began to get annoyed, but just as suddenly as it appeared, it flew off again. Five minutes later it came back, and I gazed upward again—just in time to get hit in the head by a couple of baby orchids! Flowers, hundreds and hundreds of them—eight thousand, to be exact—rained down on our heads in a perfumed cloud. Vanda orchids and plumeria fluttered through the air in a shower of flowers and the surprise of it, the utter beauty of it, was sensational. If we had been high-spirited before, we were really on top then, and it wasn't till Myron Floren got on the mike and urged us to gather round the fountain that everybody calmed down a little. Gazing at the green and rolling hills surrounding us, the beautiful new buildings behind us, and the brass fountain sparkling in the afternoon sunshine, Myron smiled and said very gently, "Lawrence—it's a long, long way from that sod farmhouse."

"This is a happy day for all of us," he added, while I groped in my pocket for my hankie. "We're all here because we love you, Lawrence. We're awfully glad you made it—and thanks for taking us along for the ride."

Then he asked Brett and State Senator

William Craven to come up and help me unveil the statue. As we tugged at the nylon covering, Myron said, "We dedicate this statue and this theater-museum to the joy and happiness of all the people who made it possible!" "Amen," I thought to myself, giving one final tug to the covering, and suddenly it fell aside and balloons, hundreds of them, escaped into the clear air, soaring up into the blue, looking— to me, anyway—like giant champagne bubbles. And there in the foreground was the bronze statue itself, shining in the rays of the sun and looking so lifelike I couldn't believe it. I thought back to that uncomfortable day with straws in my nose and goop on my face and realized what a small price it was to pay for such a fine piece of work. I also realized for the first time what a truly gifted artist Brett is. He had done a remarkable job—even my hands holding the baton looked real. I picked up another baton and hopped up beside it, striking the same pose, and the TV and newspaper photographers moved in for pictures. A few minutes later, Larry and his son Lawrence Welk the Third hopped up beside me and, with four Welks together, photographers really got busy.

The rest of the day is rather a blur to me. After the dedication, we all went into the theater to see the movie and that, as I mentioned, was an overwhelmingly emotional experience for me. Just entering the theater itself was rather over-whelming—it is large, and shaped rather like a shell, its off-white walls making a dramatic contrast to the three hundred burgundy-red continental-style seats. Two huge baskets of flowers stood at either side of the stage in front of the golden-beige curtain, and it was really so beautiful I couldn't help comparing it to the empty feed stores and farm machinery buildings that served as theaters when I first started out. Even Ted Lennon, who is usually pretty matter-of-fact, got tears in his eyes looking at the stage. "This is really something, Lawrence," he whispered. "Look at what you've accomplished." "Not me, Ted," I said. "It's you—and all the others who have been with me through the years." Then, settling back into the comfortable seats, I grabbed Fern's hand and held tight as the picture opened with a color shot of our Musical Family of today, and then changed to black-and-white as it retraced our life, starting from that little farmhouse back in Strasburg, North Dakota, in 1903. I'm in no position to be objective, I guess, but to me the picture seemed very warm, very moving. I've seen it several times since, and each time it ends, to the strain of "My North Dakota Home," I find myself swallowing hard and wiping away tears.

A lot of the audience was sniffing openly, too, when it ended. Laurie's eighteen-year-old son, Larry Rector, told me, "You know I always used to think of you as just my mother's boss. But now—gosh, you've lived the American dream!"

That long and loving day ended with a banquet in the restaurant and, in a way, that was the most fun of all. The tensions and worry over whether everything would come off as planned dissipated completely in a feeling of euphoria that everything had gone so well. Ted emceed the dinner party and, just as I had been deeply proud of Larry when he had handled things so smoothly at the screening in the theater, I now felt the same kind of pride in Ted. We had a wonderful time, but it was after dinner that we had the most fun of all. Joey Schmidt, our young resident accordionist, stepped up to the podium to entertain, and when he announced he would play one of Myron Floren's specialties, "Dark Eyes," Myron immediately pushed back his chair, walked to the front of the room, and stood directly in front of Joey, arms crossed, listening intently to every note. That was hard enough on poor Joey, but when he launched into a second chorus, Myron dragged up a chair and sat down to listen! We all roared with laughter as Joey struggled on, and when he finished, we all jumped to our feet—Myron included—and gave him a standing ovation. But that was just the beginning. Sam Lutz jumped up to suggest we thank Ted for putting together such a smash success—so we gave Ted a standing ovation. Then Ted got up and suggested we offer my secretary Lois Lamont a special vote of thanks for "sticking with the boss for thirty-four years"—and we gave Lois a standing ovation. But the topper came when I rushed up to the podium to say thanks to everyone—and got a standing ovation before I could open my mouth! I just took a bow and sat down again.

What a lucky man. What a lucky, lucky man!

3. You're Never Too Young!

When Prentice-Hall first asked me to write this book and share my secrets of happiness with those of us who have passed our thirty-ninth birthdays, I got a little insulted. "Why are you asking me?" I demanded. "I'm not old—at least I don't feel old!"

"That's just it," they said. "You seem to have discovered the secret of youth and health and happiness, and we want you to tell us what it is!"

Well, about "youth" I don't know—it's been so long ago I can't remember! But I do know I feel better and happier right now, at the age of seventy-eight, than at any other time in my life. And if the simple daily regimen and philosophies I have been following all these years are the reason for this, then I'm more than happy to share them with you. All I can tell you is they

40

have worked very well for me.

I do want you to know that the years after sixty-five can be amazingly sweet. They call them the golden years, you know, and now I'm finding out why. The pains and frustrations of the earlier years seem to become muted and eased with the passage of time and perhaps the gaining of a little wisdom—and the joys become deeper and sweeter. It is a truly wonderful time of life.

When I didn't retire at the age of sixty-five, a good many people assumed it was because I was worried that my Musical Family might suffer if I did so. And to a certain extent that's true. But the truth is *I* would suffer too! I love my work so much, a vital part of my life would simply be taken away from me if I were forced to retire. (There are certain advantages to being your own boss. Nobody can fire you.)

And I truly believe we have done some of our best work in the years since I turned sixty-five. We've improved the orchestra to the point where it can play any kind of music, and play it so well I'm in a permanent state of goose pimples. We've found several talented young newcomers, and nurtured their development into stardom. We've built a network of fans and friends larger and more loyal than ever before in our history, and none of that could have been accomplished if I had retired thirteen years ago.

So, for me anyway, continuing to do work I love is a great joy. Of course I've always believed in the power of work, as those of you who have read my other books undoubtedly know. Actually, what I really believe in is Freedom—and that includes the right to work, by anyone, at any time, at any age they wish! I have long been championing the right of our young folks to work whenever they wish (and more about that later!). But I also believe the same right should apply to those of us in our older years. That's because work does more than help you earn a living. It gives your days a meaning, a focus, a sparkle—gives you something to live for. It may even *keep* you living!

I learned that lesson years ago when I was a young man on the farm back in Strasburg, North Dakota. It was the custom then for farmers to turn over the farm to their eldest son or daughter whenever the child married, and then retire to a life of ease in town. These farmers were, generally speaking, in their early fifties at the time—in the prime of life, some of them so strong they could throw a horse or a bull. But after a few years of sitting around reminiscing with old friends in the corner grocery store, or shooting a few games of pool in the pool hall, they would begin to lose their incentive for living. Before long you'd see them shuffling down the street instead of striding along, their shoulders bent as if bearing the weight of the world, and within a few years many of them would simply wither away. Even then I was convinced that if they had kept up their daily physical labor and stayed engrossed in the business of running their farms, they would have lived many, many more years. It's an old axiom, I suppose, but true: "If you don't use it, you lose it!"

I was pleased to read recently in *Time* magazine that the most recent scientific studies support this same theory, and there is now physiological proof that consistent work and exercise not only keep your muscles young and supple, but your brain also! (I was really glad to read that—I get a little worried about my brain now and then.) The consensus of the most recent advice of specialists seems to be "Rust out—don't rest out."

Actually, I think we've known that for

many years. Marcus Tullius Cicero, a very active gentleman who lived a couple of thousand years ago, knew it when he wrote his famous essay on aging. He was eighty-four years old when he wrote that he would rather be an old man for a shorter length of time than be an old man before he was one! My sentiments exactly. I would rather keep as busy, as involved, as active as I can for as long as I can, because I believe it helps keep you young in mind and body, and I intend to stay that way as long as the Good Lord allows me to.

When we taped our final show of the 1980-81 season last February, it was certainly an active day and a long one that started at five in the morning. I got up, had my swim, breakfasted with Fern, and then picked up Henry Cuesta, our clarinet virtuoso, on my way in to the studio, something I do every Tuesday. On this particular morning, however, Henry came dashing out with a lunch sack in his hand. "Little Henry went to school early for band practice," he said, anxiously, "and he forgot his lunch. Can we drop it off at his school?"

"Sure," I said, and we drove a few blocks to the school, where Henry jumped out, dashed into the building, and came dashing out two minutes later, his eyes sparkling. "You've gotta come in, Mr. Welk," he said. "There are about eighty kids in there and they are just so cute!"

I went in and sure enough, there were about eighty little children, each one beaming widely and each holding an instrument ranging from the clarinet of ten-year-old Henry Cuesta Junior, to flutes, piccolos, and drums. Well, what could I do? I grabbed a baton, and for the next few minutes the kids and I had a wonderful time together.

After that, Henry and I jumped back in the car, drove to my office, transferred into Russ Klein's big car (he is one of our super saxophone players), picked up George Cates and my secretary Laurie, and drove crosstown to ABC to begin the morning's. rehearsal.

The show that day was a complicated one, involving a lot of staging—a wearing show in many ways, and I welcomed the lunch break at one o'clock. (I traditionally take a quick snooze at lunch instead of eating—could that be a secret?) At two o'clock we began the afternoon rehearsal—making changes, restaging and relighting the scenes. It is hard, hard work but—to me, anyway—absolutely fascinating. At five-thirty we did our dress rehearsal in front of a studio audience, and at eight o'clock we taped the show. And about nine-thirty we met backstage for a cast party to celebrate the last show of the season.

My managers, Don Fedderson and Sam Lutz, do this for us every year, and this year they had set up two long buffet tables in one corner of a huge shadowy area backstage. It looked very dramatic, really, with scenery flats stacked up against the wall, huge arc lights hanging from the ceiling grid, props in every corner, and all the band instruments neatly stacked together in their special carrying cases. (I might just tell you that all the fellows in the band take care of their musical instruments as if they were babies. They not only buy the finest they can find, they also polish them, clean them, and pack them tenderly in their cases. Our cellist, Ernie Ehrhardt, recently spent five hundred dollars on a six-foot-long, lemon-yellow carrying case to hold his big cello. Inside it is filled with velvet-covered foam rubber carved out to fit exactly the measurements of the cello. The fellows kid him that it looks like a lemon-yellow casket, but Ernie doesn't care. He just wants the best protection he can find for his priceless cello, and it warms my heart that the fellows care so very much about their profession.)

But to get back to the party . . . the buffet tables were covered with hot dogs, chili, onions, all kinds of hors d'oeuvres and salads, soft drinks, beer and wine. (I settled for a glass of ice water and a dish of macaroni salad. I eat simply!)

It was a "family" party in every way. Niki and Tom Mareschal, our long-time set photographers, brought their three-month-old baby, Shannon, a beautiful little girl. I held her and cuddled her, and danced with her, and she seemed to love it, but as I confided to one of my friends, three-month-old babies are just about the only "babies" who want to cuddle by me these days. Anacani brought her tall and handsome lawyer husband, Rudolfo Echeverria; Dick and Mary Lou Maloof brought Mary Lou's nice parents, Helen and Ernie Metzger; and Ava Barber's husband, Roger Sullivan, who is such a help on tour, came too. We all thanked each other for the privilege of working together for another year—for a few of us it marked over thirty years of togetherness—until Jim Hobson grabbed the mike and announced that if we would settle down in the studio seats he would show us a special film he had put together just for us. It turned out to be a collection of choice scenes from our old television shows, going clear back into the Lennon Sisters years, and we all laughed at the old-style clothes and hairdos, and roared with affectionate laughter at the way Dick Dale and Barney Liddell looked like their own kid brothers in some of the early shows. We were in such high good humor that by the time Tom Netherton flashed on the screen, singing from a blimp which seemed to be flying over Escondido, everyone began cheering and whistling with such insistence that Tom finally got up, made a gracious bow, and announced he was willing to sign a few autographs!

By the time I got home that night, after delivering everybody back to their respective cars and houses, it was well after midnight. But I wasn't tired, I was exhilarated. Next morning I was in the office as usual at seven o'clock, and the following morning left for a ten-day tour across the southern United States.

My point is that if I had retired thirteen years ago, I don't believe I would have had the stamina to put in such a long day. More to the point, I might not have lived long enough to do it!

So, for those of us who truly enjoy our work, I might suggest keeping on with it, at least to some degree. I did try staying home one day last April, just to see what it would be like. I slept late, had breakfast, went back to bed for another little snooze, got up, hit a few golf balls, tried to read, tried to watch TV, tried to take another nap. No go. I thought of something I could call the office about, but it turned out they had already done it. I decided to make a few phone calls, but everyone I thought of calling was busy at work and wouldn't have appreciated just chatting. By lunchtime I was so bored with myself I could hardly stand it, and by the end of the day I had learned my lesson—I'm far happier with something to do. A life without demands, without a need, something that requires our effort as well as our presence, is a life that soon loses its savor. If not a regular job, then a hobby or some interest so engrossing it will demand your attention every day.

And you're never too young to start

planning for your future interests. I'm indebted to Bernice's friend Trudy Kallis for this thought. When Bernice was first telling her about this book, Trudy said, "Well, everybody will be interested in it because we're all going to get older—if we're lucky, that is—and we're never too young to start thinking about it."

She has a point. I think most of us do make specific plans as to insurance, health benefits, and the like. But few of us formulate any plans for a life-style that will help us get the most out of life as we move along. I was lucky—I did so without even being aware of it when I saw those farmers in Strasburg, retiring early and fading away without a daily goal to keep them going. I must have resolved at some deep interior level not to let that happen to me, because here I am at seventy-eight, still working and loving it.

I will keep on working as long as I'm able. If I can't make music, then I'll write books—or coach young people—or campaign to bring back the Big Bands—or make it legally possible for young people to get the work experience they need—or entertain folks who are lonely or in despair. But I'll do something! I'll find a goal, *make* a goal—and then work to achieve it. I believe that work is one of the secrets of a happy life, and the need for it does not diminish as we grow older.

4. Exercise More . . . Eat Less!

In spite of having a terrible sweet tooth all my life, I've never had any real problems with my weight except for one time early in my career when my little band and I were playing in Big Springs, Texas. At that time, I ate so much my weight ballooned up to two hundred and four pounds. When I got a look in the mirror I didn't like myself at all and went on a rigid diet immediately. Then, just to make sure I would lose those extra pounds, I sold my car and walked everywhere for the next month! It was a drastic cure, but it worked.

It appears most of us seem to do better if we're a little underweight, rather than over, especially as we get older, so when I turned sixty-five I decided to lose one pound a year from then on. I'm still doing it and now weigh one hundred and fifty-five. (If I live a whole lot longer, I may have to reverse my plan and start *gaining* a pound a year!)

Diet and exercise do seem to play an extremely important role in our happiness and well-being, and if you were to ask me how to stay fit, I think I could answer you in just four words: "Exercise more . . . eat less!"

My own diet is very simple and was more or less forced onto me when I was recovering from a whole series of illnesses about twenty years ago. After two hospitalizations, nothing seemed to agree with my nervous tummy. I couldn't keep anything down. Finally, one of the doctors said, "Lawrence, this is something you're going to have to work out for yourself. We can't do it for you. You start making a list of everything you eat, and when you find something that disagrees with you, then don't eat it—ever!"

Fern and I started keeping records of what I ate, and before long a clear pattern began to emerge. I could easily tolerate bland, easy-to-digest foods, but anything fried, greasy, spicy, rich, or raw was off my list! Fern is a marvelous cook and she found ways to bake or broil delicious chicken or meat dishes using little or no salt or spices; these dishes, combined with cooked fruits and vegetables, make up the heart of my diet. When I'm at the studio I nibble all day on milk, tea with honey, a dish of yogurt, rice pudding or custard, or perhaps a hard-cooked egg or banana and—I must admit—cookies! I still have that sweet tooth. But whatever I eat is easy to digest. This diet seems to work very well for me and gives me the energy I need. People sometimes ask me where I get all my energy, wondering if I take some kind of super "youth" pill or injections of any kind. Folks—I wouldn't know a super pill if it came up and talked to me! Of course, I do take a little Geritol and Serutan.

Actually, food has become relatively unimportant to me in recent years. I eat because I know I should, but I don't get the pleasure out of it I once did. On the other hand, I thoroughly enjoy exercising. I love to slide into my swimming pool every morning and swim a few laps in that cool, invigorating water. And I love to play golf. I have my own little group of golfing pals at the Bel Air Country Club—Eddie Shipstad, who founded the Ice Follies; Judge Ed O'Connor, an old friend from North Dakota; Harry Franklin, my Bel Air pal;

and sometimes Mike Douglas, or Paul Weston, the composer-conductor. None of us, except for Mike and Paul—(they're just a couple of kids)—will ever see seventy again, but we compete as ferociously as if we were twenty-year-olds competing in the Masters' Pro-Am. And we have a wonderful time. Golf is a great health builder. I've even gone so far as to say it saved my life when I had a near collapse in 1957. When we first went on national television in 1955, the stress was tremendous, and when we added a second hour-long talent show a couple of years later, the stress got even greater. After a couple of seasons, I began to develop splitting headaches, stomach pains, sleepless nights, etc., and the doctors told me that unless I gave up my show they wouldn't be responsible for my life. Well, my show *is* my life, so I knew I couldn't do that. Instead, I began delegating some of my responsibilities to Jim and Myron and George Cates, and then I forced myself to go out on the golf course and get some fresh air and relaxation. The benefits were immediately apparent. Not only did my health improve dramatically, but so—I'm almost sorry to say—did the show! It was a lesson to me that no one is indispensable, and it set the scene for the policy I have followed ever since. I reserve the right to make any last-minute changes before we tape the show, if necessary, but turning the show over to my right-hand people—little by little and more and more each year—has freed me from all but the most pleasurable aspects of my work, and has developed the already great talents of my staff. So from almost every point of view, I feel I owe a great deal to golf.

In addition to golf and swimming, I also do occasional floor exercises to keep my back flexible. (I have one of those trick backs that goes out on occasion and I have some specially designed exercises to keep it under control.) Sometimes when I consider my medical history, I marvel that I'm even here today! I nearly died when I was eleven from a burst appendix, suffered for years with an irritable colon, and underwent so many surgeries and illnesses when I was in my mid-fifties that I despaired of ever reaching sixty. My good health today seems like a miracle to me, and I'm so deeply grateful for it. I'm sure all the diet and exercise and discipline involved helped achieve it. But I'm also sure the Good Lord had a hand in it, too.

And in a strange way, the very profession that sometimes gives me my nervous tummy turns out to be good for me! Just recently Phyllis Battelle wrote a column headlined, "If you want to live a long life, lead a band!" It went on to say that band leaders—symphony conductors in particular —often live into their eighties and nineties, men like Stokowski, Toscanini, Arthur Fiedler. The reason seems to be that waving your arms around in the air as we conductors do hour after hour is excellent for your heart and circulation. When I read the column, I immediately called another eager arm-waver, George Cates, into my dressing room, and he was delighted, too. But then I started to feel guilty. Here I've devoted my entire life to this profession only because I love it so much. Now it turns out it's good for me, too! How lucky can one man get?

But if I had to choose the one exercise that pays the greatest dividends in health and just plain fun, I would have to say —dancing.

5. Dancing

You think I'm kidding? Well I'm not. I get more exercise, more pleasure, more pure fun out of dancing than anything else. There's something about dancing that really keeps you on your toes, both figuratively and literally, and it's wonderful exercise. I'd a lot rather do a strenuous polka than touch my toes twenty times every morning, and the effect is just about the same.

You may notice that I dance with little Mary Lou Metzger after almost every show. (It's okay, friends—her husband, Richard Maloof, our wonderful bass player, has given me permission to do so.) I love to dance with her because she's such a wonderful little dancer she makes *me* look good! But she's not the only one. I've had the good fortune of dancing with some other very lovely ladies and fine dancers over the years—little Cissy King was an exceptionally beautiful dancer, and so was Barbara Boylan. And those of you folks who remember Alice Lon may also remember what a fine dancer she was.

On the other hand, I've had my share of *not*-so-fine dancers, too! I've already told the story of how a lady shoved through the crowd of people waiting to dance with me on our TV show one day, but instead of tagging me gently on the shoulder, she hit me so hard I nearly fell down. Then she grabbed me the wrong way and started plowing through the crowd like a steamroller. We staggered around for a couple of minutes until she said, sourly, "Mr. Welk, on television you look like a much better dancer!"

Then there was the lady who came up to me at the Palladium and begged me to dance with her mother. Since she herself was in her seventies, I had a few qualms, but she was so nice I followed her meekly to the corner of the ballroom and met her mother, a delightful little lady in her nineties. We started off in a sedate waltz, but after only a few steps she looked up at me and said, "Oh, I could just die." I hope she meant it as a compliment.

Another "young lady," who was exactly one hundred years old, said she wanted to waltz with me one time during the warm-up before our TV show. She looked so fragile I was a little nervous, but I needn't have been because she knew exactly what she was doing. When Myron broke into the "Anniversary Waltz," she listened for a moment and then said, crisply, "Play a slower tempo, young man." "Yes, ma'am," he said meekly, and started playing more slowly. After a moment she lifted her eyes to me and said, "All right, Mr. Welk. We may begin." I felt like a schoolboy, but I did as she said, and it turned out she was a beautiful dancer.

I find that the young girls of today don't know how to dance—that is, they don't know how to dance the waltz or the polka or the fox-trot I love so much. I just can't understand why today's youngsters jiggle around by themselves. Half the fun—well, most of the fun of dancing—is the chance to get a beautiful girl in your arms, and I wouldn't trade that for any of today's dances.

One of the reasons I like to go to Welk Village so often is because I get a chance to dance, especially now that Joey Schmidt plays for dancing in the lounge of our restaurant. It's wonderful fun, and sometimes I even find a lady who can do the polka. The residents enjoy dancing, too. One of them, a youngster named Alec Morris, used to teach "round dancing" to his fellow residents in one of the club-houses—in fact, Alec and his wife, Yvette, appeared on our television show one time leading a group of our kids through the steps. Perhaps you saw him. I might tell you that Alec is eighty-one and he not only has wonderful dancing feet, he swims, bowls, and plays golf and tennis regularly! If you wonder why I suggest that exercise and dancing are good ways to keep young and healthy, don't look at me, look at Alec. He's proof positive.

6. Don't Forget!

I have to laugh when I think of handing out advice here as if I were some kind of professor or teacher. I've only had four years of schooling. But you'll notice I said "laugh." If there's one thing you need for a happy life as you get older, it's a sense of humor. Of course you need it all through life. I would never have made it in this business if I hadn't been able to laugh instead of cry at some of my early reviews. Otherwise, they would have just wiped me out completely. I remember one lady who advised me to throw my accordion in the river, and another critic who said that to him our Champagne Music sounded like a poor grade of beer. My boys were incensed, but I just thought it was funny. The ability to laugh at yourself is tied in closely with humility. Humility has been defined as knowing the truth about yourself, and in that sense, humility and a sense of humor are closely aligned. After all, if you know the truth about yourself, you *better* have a sense of humor!

And I think it becomes even more important as you grow older. When your hair starts to thin, and your waist starts to thicken, and your golf drives keep getting shorter, and you can't remember things the way you used to, well, don't cry—laugh!

I might as well make a real confession right here. My memory is just not what it used to be. In fact, the reason I dragged my feet a little over writing this book is not because I was insulted that Prentice-Hall was classing me as a senior citizen. No, it was because I was afraid I wouldn't remember anything long enough to get it into print. Oh, I'm kidding, but the truth is I don't remember things the way I used to.

It bothered me terribly when I first realized this, because I used to have a very good memory. I'm not bragging, because I wasn't even aware of it at the time. But I used to do all the booking for the band myself, and I never had to refer to my route book to check on which date we were playing where. If somebody asked me where we'd be on March 12 or September 9, I could tell them immediately not only where we were going to play, but what the guarantee and our percentage of the gross would be. And I used to have a very good memory for names and faces, too. Once I met you I just didn't forget you. I used to get a kick out of standing up on the platform and seeing somebody dance toward me and call out, "Well, hello there, Joe (or Frank or whatever)! What are you doing here after all these years?" "Joe" would be absolutely amazed, and delighted that I remembered him, and it was fun for both of us. But I wouldn't advise your testing me on that these days. Chances are I not only won't remember your name, I'll have trouble recalling what town we're in.

Well, as I say, I enjoyed a clear, retentive memory all my life till about ten years ago, and then it sneaked up on me so gradually I was scarcely aware of it. It is sneaky, this memory thing, you know—and if you're my age you probably *do* know! First, you can't remember a name you've known all your life, no matter how hard you try. Two hours later, when you don't care, it suddenly comes to you. Then you can't remember whether you actually turned the

64

water off, or fed the dog, or whatever. The day you forget to give your wife an important message, the truth dawns. You just don't have the memory you used to.

I began working out my own little system to help me get around this problem, and I found that one of the best things to do is write little notes to yourself. This is absolutely foolproof—as long as you can remember where you left the notes. I also double-check everything with Fern and the girls in the office. All of them have been a great help reminding me ever so gently of this appointment or that. (They each remind me separately of the same thing, figuring, no doubt, that a mass attack has the best chance of success.) The staff on our show does the same thing, so my undependable memory is not quite the burden it would be otherwise.

And I never forget the really important things. I've yet to forget a rehearsal or the show or mass on Sunday or a golf game. It's the little daily incidentals that trip me up—like what I had for lunch . . . or *if* I had my lunch—or where I put my glasses. It's funny—I can remember vividly and in great detail what happened forty or fifty or sixty years ago. But five minutes ago—

I'm in trouble!

I'm not the only one. My manager, Sam Lutz, confesses that he not only has a little trouble now, he had *big* trouble years ago when he was manager for the Henry Busse band. That was back in the thirties, when Sam was still a very young man. One night he took the cash receipts from several one-night stands—some four thousand two hundred dollars—sealed the money inside an envelope, and tucked it under his pillow for safekeeping. Next morning he forgot all about it, got up, dressed, and climbed aboard the band bus with everybody else as it rolled out of Columbus, Ohio, on the way to the next engagement. About one hundred and thirty miles out of town he suddenly turned pale and screamed *"Stop the bus!"* When the startled bus driver pulled to a stop, Sam burst out the door and started racing to the nearest pay phone, with Henry Busse racing right beside him. Sam called the police department in Columbus and spent the next forty-five minutes pacing up and down, waiting for the policeman to call back. Mr. Busse paced right alongside him, reminding him at frequent intervals that since Sam had lost the money, Sam was the one who would have to make it up. "And

66

at thirty-five dollars a week," says Sam ruefully, "I figured it would take the rest of my natural life." The story has a happy ending, though. The policeman called back to report they had found the cash intact and would send it on to Sam. Sam sacrificed a couple of weeks' pay and sent a nice reward to the policeman—and he never forgot his money after that.

Don Fedderson was listening to this conversation and he chuckled that when he himself was just starting out in business, he met James Farley, the United States postmaster who was famous for knowing thousands and thousands of people by their first names. "How do you remember them, Mr. Farley?" asked Don eagerly. Farley explained that when he heard someone's name for the first time, he immediately associated it with a mental picture. For example, for the name Fedderson, one might think of a feather and the sun.

Don was so excited by this concept he decided to put it into practice on his very next appointment, which happened to be with a most important man named Eel. You guessed it. When Don said good-bye, he smiled winningly and said, "Thank you so much, Mr. Fish!"

Ed Kletter, our sponsor, took a similar kind of memory course one time, and when he met a man named Henhauser, he noted that in German it means "chicken house." Naturally, when they parted, Ed said cheerfully, "Well, nice to have met you, Mr. Chicken House!" But I think he really topped himself the day he graduated from his memory course. He got the highest score of anyone in his class, but when he walked across stage to pick up his diploma, he forgot his teacher's name.

So I guess we all have our problems, and bad as my memory has gotten, it's still not as bad as that of a gentleman I read about just the other day, who says his memory has gotten so bad he can't remember whether he ate his breakfast, brushed his teeth, or took his pills. So he's worked out a system. If his toothbrush is damp, chances are he's brushed his teeth. If his coffee cup is warm, he's already had his coffee; and if the pills roll all over the floor because the bottle cap is loose, he's probably taken his pills.

So I guess I'm not so bad off after all.

7. Helping Young People

One of the ways to enrich our lives the most is to help others—especially young people. It always seems to bring such great happiness. That holds true all through life, of course, but somehow in our senior years it becomes even more rewarding. For one thing, we older folks know a little more at this time in our lives—or we should!—and we have more to convey to our young friends in the way of experience and knowledge. For another, helping a young person get started not only helps *him,* it helps the whole nation. And on top of everything else, just being around young people puts a glow into your life you can't get any other way. I absolutely love working with the young singers and performers on our show. Their enthusiasm is so high, they're hungry to learn, and they're always willing and eager to try anything new.

I've been lucky that my work has allowed me to help several young people over the years: the Lennon Sisters, the Semonski family, Buddy Merrill, Bobby Beers (back in the days before television)—a whole parade of talented youngsters. In these last few years, we've found little Sheila and Sherry Aldridge; our twins, David and Roger Otwell; Kathie Sullivan; Jim Turner; and Gail, Ron, and Michael, our new trio. I want to tell you Gail's story—she's not a newcomer to the show, but she was certainly a youngster when we found her —but first I'd like to tell you the story of a young man who was not only a great challenge, but also one whose success brought me much joy. I'm talking about Joey Schmidt, and I think working with him was especially meaningful because it reminded me vividly of the years George T. Kelly had worked with me. I'd like to tell you his story right now.

Joey

Joey is a young neighbor of mine from North Dakota and in many ways he reminds me of the young Lawrence Welk. Like me, he's from a small town—Napoleon, about fifty miles from my hometown of Strasburg. Like me, he's from a close-knit, religious family, and is basically very shy. But unlike me, he was able to transform himself from a tongue-tied young accordionist into a smooth and easy talker in just one short year, while I'm still working on it!

If Joey was shy and barely able to talk when he first flew into town for his initial appearance on our show, it was certainly understandable. He was only about seventeen, maybe eighteen, and it was his first trip to a city as large as Los Angeles. He didn't appear to be too nervous during the day as we rehearsed, but when I told him he and I would chat a little on-camera during the show, he turned pale. I really felt for him—I remember how scared I had been the first time I had to talk! Somehow I had gotten through it and so did Joey. As far as his accordion playing went, he was wonderful, and I remember thinking that his technique was phenomenal, especially for one so young.

He had been brought to my attention originally by my old pal Mike Dosch, the "Resident Accordionist Supreme" of Strasburg, and also by my nephew Jimmy Schwab. Jimmy gave me a tape cassette of Joey's playing one time when I was home on a visit, and as soon as I returned to California I played it. It knocked me out to the extent that I got on the phone right away and called him. Apparently this caused a little excitement in the Schmidt household. Joey wasn't home when I called, so, as he tells it: "My Dad answered the phone and he recognized your voice right away. You kept saying 'Hello? Hello?' —but Dad was so excited he couldn't answer you! When I came home and he told me you had called, I couldn't believe it. And when you called back and invited me to be on the show, I couldn't believe that either. I was so excited I could have flown out to California right there, under my own power!"

During the next few months, as I got to know Joey better, I discovered many similarities between us. He had been born into a musical family, just as I had, and was only about three years old when he first displayed an interest in music. He was watching his mother, Helen, play her accordion, and he got out a glass quart jar and tried to imitate her. (I began playing the family pump organ at about the same age.) Joey's mother taught him some simple tunes, and when he was five she gave him his first real accordion. (I had to wait till I was seventeen for mine, although I had a series of small, very cheap accordions when I was younger.) By the time Joey was twelve, he was studying with Emil Dokter of Bismarck, and playing in the family band—his mother on piano, father Ray on accordion, older sister Ellene on sax or clarinet, younger sister Jolinda beating the drums, and Joey playing whatever was needed—he could play just about any instrument. The Schmidts were quite popular in the neighborhood, but played mainly for older crowds, so as Joey got into his teenage years he began organizing dances for the younger folks. He would rent a hall, put up advertising fliers, and hire a little rock and roll band for the kids. I laughed when he told me about it. It reminded me vividly of my own youthful ventures along that line, especially the first dance I ever promoted. That was at Hague, North Dakota, over fifty years ago. I rented a hall (in those days it cost three dollars), cleaned it, swept it, tacked up signs all over town wherever I was allowed to, went out on the street and sold tickets myself (in some cases promising to teach the young farmers how to dance if they would buy a ticket)—and then acted as the entire band myself, standing on a little stage I created in one corner, and playing to a ballroom which was jam-packed as a result of my overzealous salesmanship! It was not only my first promotion, it was the first time I made any real money, and when I showed Father the cash next morning, I think it was the first time he considered the possibility that I might be able to earn a living in music.

Now, half a century later, here was young Joey doing much the same thing. He was also working in his father's gas station eight hours a day and had managed to save up enough money to produce a record album in which he played all the instruments himself. When he returned to Napoleon after his first appearance on our show, he sent me a copy. I was impressed not only by how well he played, but by the energy and initiative he displayed. I wrote back and invited him to make a second appearance.

As before, he played beautifully, but again he just stood stiffly and stared straight ahead into the camera looking like he was scared to death, and I wondered if he was really cut out to be a performer. But a few weeks later I got a long, very thoughtful letter from him. He wrote to say his teacher had told him there was nothing more he could teach him. "You need more advanced instruction now," he said. "I've taught you all I know."

Joey was discouraged. There weren't any advanced teachers in his area, and there weren't too many places for him to play, either, outside of a few dance dates and occasional club shows. He was still working in the gas station and that really wasn't his idea of a lifetime career. He felt stymied and at a dead end. "I wanted to play music so much I could hardly get through the day," he told me later, "and the thought of staying and working at the gas station for the rest of my life really depressed me." Again, I felt a pang of recognition. I used to worry myself sick when I was Joey's age, afraid I'd have to stay and be a farmer all my life, so when Joey wrote, pouring out his feelings of frustration and unhappiness, I could identify with him completely and understand how he felt. "I want to make something of myself," he concluded, "and since my teacher here says he can't teach me any more, I wonder if you would talk to Myron Floren and ask him if there's someone he could recommend in Los Angeles. Maybe I could come out there and study."

I put Joe's letter down and sat for a long time, thinking. I felt very strongly that he didn't need instruction as much as he needed a short course in showmanship. He had the talent and the technique and the desire—he just didn't quite know how to put himself over. I talked to Myron, who agreed with me, and then I wrote Joey and asked him if he would like to come out and work in our restaurant in Escondido. "That way you can get experience playing for different kinds of audiences, and if Myron has to go on a personal appearance some-time, perhaps we can bring you on for a show."

Joey was thrilled when he got the letter. He'd been collecting Myron's records as far back as he could remember, playing them over and over, trying to imitate him (so if his playing sounds a little like Myron's, now you know why!). The thought that he was actually getting a chance to play with his lifetime idol seemed like a dream come true.

His family hated to see their only son leave—hated to break up the family band. But they realized how limited his options were in their small town, so they helped him pack his clothes and his books and his Myron Floren records, and then Joey and his parents and two sets of aunts and uncles drove cross-country in their van.

I met them when they arrived and we hit it off immediately—our North Dakota roots reached out and pulled us all together—and then we drove on down to Escondido to get Joey safely settled. I had a long talk with his parents, who were naturally concerned about their young son moving so far away from home, and I think Joey himself was a bit nervous about starting a new life so far away. But everyone in Escondido immediately took him under their wings, and Roger and David Otwell, with whom he had become very friendly, made it a point to drive down and visit him often. In turn, Joey would drive his little blue Datsun to North Hollywood and visit the boys in their small apartment, and before long he had settled into a comfortable groove.

Nevertheless, the first time I watched him perform in the restaurant, my heart sank, and I wondered if I'd made a terrible mistake bringing him so far away from home. He was just so shy! He played beautifully, but he would come out, stand stiffly at the mike, announce his name and the numbers he was going to play, and then race through them as if anxious to get off the platform. He seemed so uncomfortable that the audience got a little uneasy, too. My heart ached for him.

I took him aside. "Joey," I said. "I think what you need to do is just relax a little—loosen up and talk more. Sort of visit with the audience—tell them where you're from, a little about your background . . . that sort of thing."

Joey nodded, listening intently to my suggestions and promising to try. Sure enough, next week when I came to Escondido for another coaching session, he was talking a little more, but three weeks later he was still very, very stiff and ill-at-ease. His own nice personality was just not coming through.

"You know what I think would help you?" I asked. "If you went from table to table playing requests for the folks, I think you would develop more ease in talking. Why don't you try that?"

Panic flared in Joey's blue eyes and he flushed beet red. "Oh, gosh, Mr. Welk," he stammered. "I—I couldn't do that!

"Why not?" I wanted to know.

"Well," he floundered, "for one thing, I play a Cordovox [an electric accordion], and I couldn't walk through the restaurant with that. I'd have to go back to my old-style accordion—and I haven't played that for a long time."

"You won't always be in places where you can play your Cordovox," I pointed out. "Maybe you better keep up your technique on your old accordion. And Joey, I have a very strong feeling that if you will just go up to people at the tables and ask for their requests, it will really help you overcome your shyness. I'd like to see you try it."

"Oh, gee, Mr. Welk," he said, miserably, "it would really bother me to go right up to people and start talking to them. I . . . I just don't think I could do that."

"Sure you can," I reassured him. "I've been in this business for fifty years and nobody has bitten me yet! The folks will love you, Joey, if you give them half a chance. Just ask them if there's a birthday or anniversary they want to celebrate—and then play 'Happy Birthday' or 'The Anniversary Waltz'—or ask them where they're from, and play their state song!"

"But I don't know any state songs," said Joey, in a small voice. "Not even North Dakota."

"Well," I said, laughing a little, "then this will give you a chance to learn them! Come on, it's easy—I'll show you." I pulled on my accordion and began going from table to table, chatting with the folks and playing their state songs. Joey followed along behind, face solemn, listening intently to every note. (I didn't write any of the songs down, but next time I came to Escondido he knew them all.)

Nevertheless, as we talked that day, I felt very worried, concerned. I was afraid maybe I had put Joey into a situation that was just too much for him. He was too fine a boy to be hurt, and I wasn't sure just how to help him. I was really worried as I began driving back to Los Angeles that afternoon.

But if I was worried, Joey was devastated! As soon as I had gone, he got into his own car and drove to the top of a nearby mountain peak where he often went when he was lonely or distressed. Now, as he sat in the deepening dusk, watching the evening shadows begin to hide the valley beneath him, all the anxiety and hopes and fears he had been holding back for weeks suddenly burst through—and Joey collapsed into sobs. He cried as if his heart would break. "I just felt I had really messed up my big chance," he told me later. "I thought . . . I'm not pleasing Mr. Welk. I haven't played my old accordion in months. And I can't go right up to people and start talking. I just *can't!*" For just a moment, on that dismal evening, Joey thought about giving up and going back to North Dakota.

After a while, however, his own natural optimism and determination began to return, and he thought, "No! I'm not gonna give up. And I'm gonna start practicing on my old accordion right now!" And he dried his tears, put the car into gear, drove back down the hill to our mobile home where he was then living, got out his accordion, and practiced till far, far into the night. Joey Schmidt was not about to give up!

Of course, I didn't know that at the time, but I did notice next time I came to

Escondido that Joey was walking from table to table, taking requests. Not only that, he was smiling shyly instead of standing poker-faced when he entertained the room as a whole. He seemed a little more confident in his speech, too, and he was certainly talking more. In fact, he was talking too much! I took him aside and suggested, as diplomatically as I could, that perhaps he should talk a little less . . . "just enough to get the folks in a relaxed mood."

Poor Joey! I don't doubt that there was more than one occasion when he felt like going back to North Dakota. In addition to his struggle to find himself at Escondido, something else was complicating his life. I became aware of it when Myron was away on a personal-appearance tour and Joey was making another guest appearance on the show. He had been thrilled when I telephoned and invited him, and every time I saw him on the day of the show, he was practicing his number. But when the show was over, he seemed very subdued, even though his solo had gone extremely well. He didn't say anything and neither did I —because I was pretty sure what the problem was. It happens very often when someone new joins our "family"—it just takes time for a newcomer to be accepted into such a close-knit group. I think that's fairly normal in most situations, and in Joey's case, some of the musicians in the band apparently thought he was much too young and inexperienced to be in the star spot, and a few of them mistook his bone-deep shyness for aloofness. Whatever it was, it caused Joey great unhappiness, and I wouldn't be surprised if he didn't shed a few more tears into his pillow that night.

But Joey had made up his mind to succeed. He stuck it out. For the next few months he concentrated on improving his technique, spending hours recording his numbers on equipment he had set up in the living room of our mobile home, listening to the playback, and then practicing some more. He kept on trying to improve his talking, too, and little by little, he did! "It gets easier every time I talk," he told me. "Now it's more like talking to a bunch of friends."

That was the key. When Joey discovered for himself that the folks in Escondido were just like the folks in Napoleon (or in Florida or Timbuktu, for that matter), his shyness disappeared. When he realized they were mothers and fathers and aunts and uncles just like the people he'd grown up with, his own warm and charming personality began to emerge. It was like watching a butterfly come out of a cocoon. Well, maybe you shouldn't say that about a young man. But Joey did seem to shake off the remnants of his shyness and stiffness, and he emerged as a self-confident, poised young man, able to joke and chat with the audience as if he'd known them all his life.

By the time we were in Escondido making our movie, Joey had made such strides in stage presence that George Cates was amazed. "I can't get over that kid," he said one day as we listened to Joey during our lunch break. "The difference is tremendous; he's just wonderful." And I think we all realized Joey had "graduated" the day Greg Killingsworth brought his parents to lunch. Now Greg's mother is a truly beautiful, blonde, and glamorous lady, and when Joey spotted her at our table he came rushing right over to see if he couldn't play something for her. When he discovered her name was Laura, he immediately launched into the song "Laura," and while we were still applauding this performance he segued over to the next table where a group of about twelve ladies were celebrating a birthday. "Well!" said Joe brightly, flashing his dimples and gazing around the table at each one of them in turn, "And what can I play for *you* lovely ladies today?" I grinned. I had a feeling my coaching sessions were drawing to a close. When I saw Joey a few weeks later, playing in the lounge of our restaurant for dancing, I was sure of it. There he was, surrounded by his beloved loudspeaking equipment, playing requests for the guests, laughing with them, joking, chatting—but never once losing his sure touch on the accordion or his control of the situation. I watched in delighted amazement for a few moments and then rushed out on the tiny dance floor myself. I had a wonderful time, but it wasn't just from the dancing, which I always love. It was my delight at Joey's progress.

Joey had made phenomenal strides in just a few short weeks, but he was still unhappy over the slight strain and coolness that existed between him and some of the fellows in the band. Suddenly, as though planned, an emergency situation solved that problem, too. Myron fell ill with hepatitis and had to be off the show for three weeks, and we needed a substitute accordionist in the band. Joey was the obvious choice—but could he handle such a tough assignment? We all knew he could play brilliant solos, but playing in an orchestra is something else again, and none of us was too sure he could handle it. It didn't take Joey long to prove that he could. He showed up early for rehearsal, arranged his music on the stand, and sat down calmly to await George Cates, and if he was nervous about working with twenty-six of the finest musicians in the business, he certainly didn't show it. George laughed, telling me about it later. "Joey reads music like a pro and follows directions perfectly. He's top-rate—I think he'll be one of the greatest."

Joey's performance was a revelation to the rest of the band. I don't think any of them had realized the extent of his formal training or the depth of his musical knowledge, and at the end of the first session many of them came over to congratulate him and tell him what a great job he had done. That made Joey feel wonderful. The second week was a repeat of the first, and by the end of those three weeks any strain, any awkwardness, had vanished completely in a warm tide of acceptance. Joey had proved himself and had become—truly—a member of the family.

He had made stunning progress in less than a year. From a tongue-tied youngster so scared he could scarcely open his mouth, he had grown into a poised performer and a musician able to take his place with the rest of the band. And if there was any doubt about it, it disappeared when we went to Sun City, Arizona, to play a concert in the beautiful Sundome Center for the Performing Arts.

The show went very well, but after about two and a half hours the applause began to die down a little, as is natural after that length of time. And it was at this difficult spot I called on Joey. "Folks," I said, as he walked out on stage, "this is Joey Schmidt, a young neighbor of mine from North Dakota." Then I took a look at him and said, "Joey—why don't you tell the folks about yourself?" And I just turned the stage over to him.

So there he stood, on his own in front of nine thousand people, blond hair gleaming in the overhead lights, dimples flashing, eyes sparkling—and he began to talk, easily, fluently, even throwing in a little joke or two. All those weeks and months of coaching, all the hours of struggling to talk to the audience in the restaurant, all the long, hard hours of daily practice were really paying off—because Joey brought the house down. He played not one, not two, but three encores, and the applause was just as great at the end as at the beginning. Watching him take a graceful bow, watching him float offstage on a tremendous cushion of applause, I couldn't help but remember the scared and tongue-tied youngster who had mumbled a few words and raced through his solos only a few short months before. He had faced tremendous odds and won, and I felt a wave of great admiration and affection for Joey wash over me. I've always had an urge to help people—especially those who try to help themselves. Joey had never given up, and he had really come through.

I couldn't have been prouder of him, and I would like to go on record right now as saying that if Joey sticks to the path he has laid out for himself, and continues to work, he will become one of the greatest accordionists the world has ever known. I'm just happy that my Musical Family and I had a small hand in it.

A Year of Miracles

When Michael Redman of our wonderful new team of Gail, Ron, and Michael was telling me of the momentous things that had happened to him in the year before he joined our show, he said simply, "It was a year of miracles." As I listened, I learned that Michael and his wife, Cinda, had been on a professional and emotional roller coaster that had plunged them into some very, very low spots during that year, and then soared very high. And it was of great joy to me to learn that we turned out to be the "high."

Originally I had planned to tell Gail's story only, as one of the best examples I've ever encountered of the power of faith, persistence, and a positive attitude. Those are three qualities that serve us well at any age, whether you're as young as Gail or as old as her boss! But Gail's story is so intertwined with that of Ron and Michael, I decided to tell all three.

Gail

I imagine many of you folks remember when she first joined our show about ten years ago—a fresh-faced little girl from Durant, Oklahoma. I didn't know much about her except that she had a pleasant, true voice, was a pretty youngster, and came from a solid, southern religious background. But I loved her attitude! When I explained to her that we couldn't guarantee her any solos when I first hired her, it didn't bother her one bit. "Oh, that's okay," she assured me blithely, big blue eyes sparkling. "I don't care. Just being on this show is enough—like going to a terrific school!"

I hadn't realized till then that she looked on me as a teacher, but that was fine with me. I've often said that practical experience tends to be far more valuable than formal schooling for certain types of people—most certainly for me—and I just don't think you can really learn anything till you actually *do* it. That may be especially true for our profession. You really can't learn how to handle yourself on stage till you actually get up there and try. At any rate, I was pleased to find this sunny little girl agreeing with my theories, and I watched with interest as she plunged into her new job with great enthusiasm.

And did she plunge! All of us soon became accustomed to the sight of Gail watching everything intently, asking questions, learning every facet of her new job. Even so, I'm sure she was a little disappointed at first. It's one thing to be told you're not going to have any solos, and quite another to come to the studio week after week and not be in the spotlight. But Gail never complained, and after a couple of months singing in group numbers, word of some of her extraordinary talents began to surface. Both George and Jim came to tell me how musically talented she was, and we were all intrigued to learn she had near-perfect pitch. For those of you who aren't musically inclined, that means she can sing a note perfectly without an instrument to give her the key. She used her gift to help the other girls rehearse when there wasn't a piano available—Gail would hit the note they needed so they could practice their song. It turned out, also, that she had had a solid musical training in college, and soon she began bringing in band arrangements good enough for us to use on the show.

And if that wasn't enough, I heard her playing the piano one day with such skill that I asked her if she'd like to try doing a ragtime act, something like the kind Jo Ann Castle had made so famous. "Sure!" said Gail, with her sparkling readiness to try anything new. She practiced for weeks, and then got together with Rose Weiss, our costumer, and hairdresser Roselle Friedland, who came up with a Jo Anne Castle-type blonde wig. When Gail got herself into that getup and played our rinky-dink piano, she was so good we featured the act in our show at Harrah's in Tahoe. After that she sang in trios, duets, quartets, or danced in group numbers, and it seemed no matter what we asked her to do, she could do it. But somehow it never seemed to bring the star spot her talents so richly deserved.

But she never stopped trying. She spent a goodly portion of her salary on weekly vocal lessons with a top coach, and before long the results were apparent, and we began using her high soprano voice to sing obbligato in many of our choral arrangements. It was about this time, too, that the Semonski Sisters came along, and I asked Gail to try writing some arrangements that would capture their youthful freshness. She did—and came through with her usual fine job.

By now it was obvious that Gail had developed a musical sophistication that was at once admired and just a little different from the rest of our show. She was newer, more contemporary, her phrasing and intonations similar to the most popular groups of the day, and her musical knowledge was unusually deep and wide-ranging. We realized that in Gail we had a potential of tremendous proportions if we would just harness her numerous talents and present them in the way that showed her off the best.

I think we did to a certain degree in the trio of Sandi, Gail, and Mary Lou. Those three lovely ladies sang so well and looked so pretty that they became very popular with our audience. But one day lovely Sandi came to me and asked if she could be excused from doing the show every week. "You know I have four children now, Lawrence," she said, "and I just don't feel right being away from them every week while they're still so young."

"Sandi," I said, taking her by the hand, "you stay with your beautiful children, and just come in and sing with us when you have the time. Your family is the most important thing in your life." Sandi's eyes filled with tears, but I meant it, and I was more than happy to accede to her request. But with Sandi more or less retired from the show, at least temporarily, and Mary Lou doing more and more specialty numbers with Jack Imel, it meant that Gail was somewhat at loose ends.

She began writing arrangements, using different groups of singers, trying to achieve a new sound, a new dimension for the show. She tried several combinations and one day came up with a group composed of herself, Larry Hooper, Charlie Parlato, Kenny Trimble, and Dick Dale. When we heard them sing, we got very excited. The blend was different, happy, very good. Gail had written some strong, upbeat arrangements, and people seemed to like the sound of her clear voice backed by the men's, but then our dear Larry became seriously ill, and without his basso profundo, the group simply didn't have the same sound. We were all deeply concerned about Larry, of course. He has most certainly suffered more than his share of illness. You may recall that he was seriously ill and off the show for four years once before. When he returned in 1973, it signaled the most joyous outbreak of cheers and applause from the studio audience I have ever heard in a lifetime in the business. He is truly loved. We all pray he will be able to rejoin us soon.

By now Gail had been with us ten years. Anyone without her optimistic, up-front attitude would have probably given up and said, "Well, okay. I guess I'll just never find the perfect group, the perfect spot." But Fate has a way of rewarding people who don't like to give up, who keep their spirits up, and do their best to achieve their dreams. And Fate was ready to reward Gail. She met her future husband, Ron Anderson.

Ron

"Yes, it really started when I met Ron," Gail told me, dimpling a little as she did. "He and I met in acting class." (As usual, Gail was extending her talents, studying acting as well as singing, dancing, and musical composition.) "We were assigned as partners, acting together in various skits," she went on, "and we became friends. That's all—just buddies. But over the next year we discovered we had similar backgrounds. I found out that Ron had graduated with a degree in music from Bethany College, in Santa Cruz, California, and earned a graduate degree from Cal State in Hayward." Gail herself has a degree and a near perfect 4.0 average—from the University of Tulsa. "Anyway, I found out he had a wonderful baritone voice and had done a lot of gospel singing—he was minister of music at a big church in northern California for a while. But when we met, he was working in various game shows—like *Password*—helping producers block out the programs, and also acting in occasional movie roles. But he wanted more than that. He wanted to sing; he had big dreams, too, just as I did, and we used to talk about them just as friends."

But on February 7, 1978 (when I talked with Ron later, he gave me the exact same date, so I know it means a lot to both of them), Ron delivered an acting-class script to Gail at the studio where we were taping the show. He thought perhaps they could rehearse a little during her lunch break. "But," says Gail, taking up the story again, "halfway through that lunch, Ron and I fell in love." "What?" I asked incredulously. "In the middle of a hamburger?" Gail laughed. "I guess so. All I know is we both discovered at practically the same moment that we felt much more strongly about each other than just friends, and from that moment on, our lives changed."

I remember Ron visiting Gail at the studio along about that time, and I sensed that they were extremely happy being together, so I wasn't too surprised when they came and told me they were going to be married. I liked Ron immensely when I met him—I liked his attitude where Gail was concerned, and I was happy that she would have someone to love and care for her.

"But," says Ron, who has a great sense of humor, in addition to his blond good looks, "even though we knew we were in love and wanted to get married, we couldn't seem to find enough free time to do it! Either Gail was booked solid with appointments, or I had a full week of commitments or something else conflicted. But one day I noticed I had a full day coming up without any appointments at all, so I wrote a note and passed it over to Gail.

'Dear Gail,' it read, 'will you marry me on Friday, December 9th?' 'Dear Ron,' she wrote back, 'I'd love to!' And we did.''

While all this was going on, Gail was also having ongoing discussions with Jack Pleis, one of our brilliant arrangers, still talking about what kind of vocal group they could put together that would give that certain added element we were looking for. (I might just say in passing that one of the things that makes me so proud of my people and so attached to them is the way they work constantly to improve the show. That's their first goal. Naturally, they'd like to be ''star of the week,'' too, but their first thought is always, Is it good for the show?) That's what Gail and Jack were talking about, and one day Gail said, ''Well, Ron has a fine baritone and our phrasing and timing are almost identical. If we could find a tenor with the same vibrato and timbre—I think we'd have a very good new sound.'' But where to find the perfect tenor? In spite of the fact that Gail knew dozens of singers from having worked in various choral groups around town, she couldn't think of exactly the right one. ''And the funny thing was,'' she says, frowning as she recalled that time for me, ''I *knew* it—I just couldn't recall the name of the person I had in mind. It will come to me," she kept reassuring Ron, "don't worry." And it did. "Just as I was driving by the corner of Sepulveda and Ventura," laughs Gail. "It was weird. The name came to me from out of the blue, just as if someone had spoken it into my ear—Michael Redman. I remembered he had sung with the Johnny Mann singers and Donny and Marie, but that's all I remember—I couldn't even recall what he looked like. But the name came to me so clearly I felt sure he was the one."

And that's where Michael Redman's year of miracles comes in.

Michael

Michael had been performing for several years as a singer and occasional dancer in shows like *Donny and Marie, Johnny Mann,* and *Red Skelton,* and doing very, very well indeed. But then, as often happens in this business, everything dried up. All three shows went off the air, and in spite of his impressive credentials and wide experience in all phases of show business, Michael couldn't seem to get anything steady, just an occasional chorus job. Show business is notoriously unstable, of course, and Michael and his wife, Cinda, had prepared themselves for just such an emergency. They figured they could get by on their savings for about two years; beyond that, the future looked bleak. But Michael, who was born in Tryon, North Carolina, and had worked and trained all his life for a career in show business, was not about to give up the dream of his life too easily. "I knew my parents would help us if we got in serious trouble," he says, "but I didn't want to do that—wouldn't do that. Both Cinda and I felt this was something we had to work out ourselves."

To add to the already complicated pressure and drama of their lives, something totally unexpected—and absolutely wonderful!—had also happened to them. In 1978, the young Redmans had adopted a beautiful infant girl, baby Jennifer. Now —two years later, as so often happens, pretty Cinda found herself pregnant. "That was the first miracle," grins Michael. They were delighted, of course, but with the prospect of a wife and *two* babies to support, Michael knew he had to be realistic about the future. "If it were just Cinda and

recognized immediately that they had a wonderful blend, and that little something extra, that star quality we're always looking for. I invited them to come back and sing again after they worked up some more songs, and they did. This time they sang "Just an Old-Fashioned Love Song," and again I was extremely pleased. (Later, Gail confessed they took a lesson from me. "You always say you do everything you can to please your audience," she informed me, "so we did everything we could to please you! We knew 'And I Love You So' was one of your favorite songs, and so was 'Just an Old-Fashioned Love Song' . . . and those were the ones we worked hardest on. We figured if you liked the songs to begin with, we would have a much better chance!" I laughed when she told me. She'd really learned her lesson well.)

I talked things over with Jim and George and Jack Pleis, and we all agreed the three of them were good enough to make a guest appearance on the first show of the new season. Since that couldn't be taped till July, I took the three of them with me on a couple of other appearances in the interim—once to the Conference of Christians and Jews dinner party, and then to the annual powwow at Indian Wells in Palm Springs where the band and I entertain every year. It turned out to be one of the nights the Palm Springs Chamber of Commerce doesn't like to talk about—cold and very, very windy. We were entertaining outdoors, and after a while the audience got so chilled and uncomfortable—as did the musicians—that we had to call the concert off early. But Gail and Ron and Michael proved themselves wonderful troupers and didn't seem to mind the uncomfortable surroundings a bit. Again, I was impressed with them.

Meanwhile, small miracles were beginning to happen for the Redman family! Gail's call had not only given Michael renewed confidence and hope, it seemed to have started the ball rolling again and extra jobs began coming along. Things improved so much by the time baby Melissa made her long-awaited appearance in May, both Michael and Cinda felt confident enough to cancel plans to sell their home and move back to Portland. Nothing was sure, of course, but somehow the Redmans were filled with a heady assurance that somehow, some way, everything was going to work out.

Gail, Ron, and Michael kept rehearsing daily, and in July they made their first appearance on the show and sang with such charm, such class, the studio audience just fell in love with them. They looked so perfect, so right together I almost hired them then and there. But I couldn't, for a variety of reasons. We were booked to play Las Vegas in August, which meant we had to tape the first show in mid-July, and wouldn't be able to tape the second till late August. On top of that, none of our new shows would be seen on television till mid-September, and since we always wait to see how the viewing audience likes our new-comers before we hire them, it meant a very long, long wait before these fine young people would find out what their future was going to be. I wanted so much to say something positive to them, but I couldn't.

Nevertheless, toward the end of August I telephoned and invited them to make a second appearance. "We were so relieved when you called," laughs Gail. "We had been on tenterhooks all those weeks, wondering if we had really made a hit with you." "And we wanted to be on the show so bad we could taste it," added Ron. "Not just to sing in the trio, but in the chorus, too—we just plain wanted to be on the show. We all have religious backgrounds and even when times are tough, we pick and choose what we want to do. Michael, for instance, wouldn't appear in any alcohol or cigarette commercials, even when he needed the work so badly. He just feels strongly against them and won't do it. But we all wanted to be part of the Welk show.''

Of course, I didn't know any of that. None of them ever put any pressure on me. They knew, as well as I, that I already had many—some say *too* many—soloists on the show, and the one thing I didn't need was two more singers! But I also knew that these three people seemed to strike a spark when they sang—not only in their singing, but in their listeners. That's why I took a chance and invited them back a second time, before we had any response from our viewers.

"We were all hoping you'd come to us after that second show and tell us we were 'in,' '' says Gail. "But you didn't . . . and neither did George, or any of the arrangers. Everybody came and told us how well we sang, and that was great, of course. But nobody came and said those magic words—'You're part of the show!' We were really depressed, very let down when we went home that night.''

Unbeknownst to Gail, however, I had a meeting with the production board next day, and we talked about how well the three of them had sung and what an exciting sound they brought to the show. ''Fellas,'' I said, ''what do you think? Do you think the audience will like them as much as we do? Shall we take a chance and go ahead and hire them now? I hate to keep them waiting so long for an answer.''

''As far as I'm concerned, you can hire them right this minute!'' said George Cates positively, and everyone else in the room agreed. ''Good,'' I said. ''George—do you want to do the honors?''

That's how it happened that Gail's telephone rang about four o'clock that afternoon. When she answered, George was on the other end of the line. (Here Gail imitates George's powerful, raspy growl.) ''Gail? Gail? Can you and the fellows come to rehearsal tomorrow morning? Are the fellows willing to sing in the choral groups as well as the trio? Can all three of you make the show every week from now on? Are you willing to do that? Are you? Are you?''

Were they! They couldn't agree fast enough, and three delirious people jumped for joy the rest of the afternoon. "Nevertheless," Ron told me, "we didn't really believe it till the next taping, when you introduced us by saying, 'I'm very happy to announce that Gail, Ron, and Michael are now regular members of our Musical Family.' I don't know when," said Ron, suddenly very serious, "I don't know when I've been happier—when we've been happier. To us it was a dream come true. The way Gail and I found each other—the way we found Michael—the way our voices blended so perfectly—the way you accepted us. I can't express my feelings properly."

Ron and Gail and Michael are all from religious backgounds, as I mentioned, and have strong family ties—and enough faith and optimism for a roomful of people. "Ron's the worrier, though, the noncalm one," says Gail, "while Michael has the faith of an angel. He's always positive things are happening for the best. While I—I guess I'm sort of in between."

I wouldn't say that. Gail has the faith of angels, too. She never gave up, not even when things seemed at a stalemate, and some of the acts and arrangements and groups she had worked so hard to put together didn't quite make it.

But now, when she and her handsome husband and their equally handsome friend stand together and sing with such style, such verve, it's obvious that the star spotlight has fallen on them at last. Our fans agree. We received over a hundred letters of approval following their first appearance, and the letters are still coming in. Yes, Gail, Ron, and Michael have come home.

To a very large extent, it happened because each of them was totally prepared—each is a good sight reader, each is totally professional and totally disciplined, and each willing to spend hours every day polishing their songs to perfection.

But if you ask Michael, that's not the whole reason they found themselves singing on our show. "There's more to it than that," he says, eyes dark with feeling. "Why did Gail suddenly find herself thinking of my name? What made her think of me—when there are hundreds of other singers in this town?" To Michael, the answer is obvious. The Good Lord himself, or one of his angels, must have whispered his name into Gail's ear.

And you know something? I don't have a whole lot of trouble believing that myself.

8. Let's Free Them

While we're talking about young people, I would like to address myself to something very, very dear to my heart, and if you've been with me through my past books—particularly the last two—you can probably guess what it is. Yes, it's about our young people and the way we have made it almost impossible for them to work.

We can see some of the sad results all around us, especially in the crime wave afflicting us today. Never before in our history have there been so many cruel and senseless crimes. I'm not going to go into them, because we all know what they are. But you and I know that in all parts of the country, people have become afraid to walk down the street, afraid to go out alone after dark, afraid to stay in their own homes.

It's a matter of record that a great

percentage of these crimes are committed by young people—unemployed young people. And I believe with all my heart that had we allowed those youngsters to work, much of this crime wave might never have happened, and certainly not to the extent it has. It just stands to reason that when we prevent a young person from working, he's going to use up his energy and brains and powerful emotions in other ways! Several years ago I wrote a pamphlet on this very subject in which I said, "Nature gave our young people a tremendous amount of energy, and if we don't help them use it properly, it is going to dam up and burst out at some weak spot which will harm us all." I still feel that way, more strongly than ever. It just seems so obvious to me that if we prevent our young people from earning an honest dollar, some of them are going to find other ways to get some money.

The problem is, as I see it, the child labor law. I've said it before and I'll say it again—that law should never have been written. Or else it should have been written so that the *employers* were punished, not the children who were abused and exploited. As it turned out, it was the children who were really punished by being deprived of their right to work.

It is especially harmful in the case of our underprivileged young people—youngsters of ten, twelve, or fourteen, jammed into ghettos, trapped in a welfare life-style, like their parents before them, with no real chance of getting out. Wouldn't it be far better to help these youngsters learn a trade as early in life as they want to, and perhaps earn a little pocket money on the side? The alternative is either spending twelve years in school (and for many young people this is sheer torture and doesn't come close to meeting their real needs), or going to a trade school and paying someone to teach them a craft. Wouldn't it be simpler and better for them to learn a trade on the job and earn a few dollars on the side while they're still young, rather than wait till they're sixteen or eighteen and then try desperately to get a job? The chances are they'll have a very difficult time, because few employers are willing to pay the full minimum wage to inexperienced, untrained young adults. I feel sure that most youngsters would be delighted to earn a few dollars and learn a trade while they are still quite young, rather than be denied the privilege of earning and learning at all.

I've noticed that some bills have been introduced into Congress lately to lower the minimum-wage requirements for teenage youngsters. That's a step in the right direction, but it would be even better, in my opinion, to remove any kind of wage minimum at all. As it stands now, it's practically reached the point where children cannot legally mow the lawn or babysit for the neighbors without their "employers" paying them the full minimum wage and filling out Social Security forms. What a waste of time, talent, and potential! One of the saddest by-products of this entire situation is the discouragement a child feels at these encounters, the loss of his childhood hopes, the feeling that there is no place in society for him. No wonder we have such grave social problems.

I talked about this situation at length in *This I Believe,* my last book. In it, I poured out my heart in the hopes I could reach people and enlist their aid in making it possible for our youngsters to work if they wanted to. I failed. The minimum-wage laws are still in effect. The child labor law is still in effect. Vast numbers of people are still employed to make sure that hundreds of thousands of young people cannot work without first submitting to a strangling network of social-service requirements, permission slips, and duplicate forms. The requirements have become so stringent they discourage most employers from even trying to hire young people, much as they might like to. I myself am somewhat in that position. I try to help as many youngsters as I can, but the miles of red tape involved, trying to adjust our rehearsal and taping schedule to meet the demands of the social-service agencies, make it just about impossible.

This nation has always provided great opportunity and encouragement to its citizens, more so than any other government in the world. That's why it pains me to see how we have kept an entire segment of our population from one of its basic rights—the right to work. In my opening chapters I said that my work gives me more joy than anything else in my life, and I honestly believe it is the main reason I have stayed healthy and vigorous as long as I have. I believe all older people should be allowed to work as long as their talents are usable and they wish to contribute to society. But it's far more important to give our youngsters that privilege. They are our future leaders, those who will carry on our name and our ideals and our strength. Allowing—even encouraging—them to work can be one of the best possible tools to help them carve out a successful future for themselves.

All my life I have believed in the power of work. Now, at the age of seventy-eight, I believe in it more strongly than ever. Recently I was browsing through a book which has given me many hours of good reading, *Here's How by Who's Who,* in which several successful leaders share their secrets of success with young people. Many of them stress one point, and I would like to share it with you. First, Tom Anderson, the editor of Farm and Ranch Publishing Company, says about work: "One of life's most rewarding blessings is work. How sad that so many people go through life doing the wrong work." M. Stanton Evans, editor of the Indianapolis *News,* lists six rules for success, and his very first rule is: "Do something you enjoy. Pick a career that suits your talent and your inclinations." And finally, our President, Ronald Reagan, said: "Get in a line of work you *like* and take any job, even sweeping floors, just to get it—and then work for your goal!"

I agree with all of them, but I'd like to

ask one question: How is a young person going to discover his talents and inclinations if he isn't allowed to work and sample different professions? That is so important! If we could help make it possible for just a few youngsters to try different jobs and find the work they love, it would be worth great effort on our part. If we could help *all* young people do that, it would be worth every effort.

I am hoping that you who read these words will give serious consideration to the idea of freeing our youngsters from the burdensome restrictions that now tie them up and hold them back. Free them to find the work that can help make their path through life happy and satisfying.

9. Raindrops

Into each life some rain must fall. That's an old saying, of course, but that's okay—I'm an old man! At any rate, it's very true, and in spite of the fact that I have had so much happiness in life, I have had my share of heartaches, too. One of these was our appearance at the MGM Grand Hotel in Las Vegas in August of 1980.

For years we played Harrah's at Lake Tahoe every summer, and that was pure pleasure all the way. Bill Harrah and I had a fine relationship, my Musical Family and I played to large and enthusiastic family audiences twice a night, and just being in Tahoe itself was wonderful. After sixteen consecutive years, however, we lost Bill during heart surgery—and somehow the spirit went out of all of us. I had had a more or less unspoken agreement with Bill during all those years not to play any other resort hotel. My family and friends and I truly enjoyed our many years at Harrah's, and we always stayed faithful to Bill. Besides, my instincts told me our audience simply wasn't in Las Vegas. It's a different crowd entirely from the one that goes to Tahoe, and I felt our family type of entertainment would be lost in that kind of environment.

But after Bill Harrah died, the pressure from the other hotels began to mount, and some of my right-hand people began to push a little, too. "Las Vegas is the entertainment capital of the world," they told me. "You should play there and let the people see what a great band you have!"

Well, it's true, I'm very proud of my Musical Family and always want to show them off. But I honestly didn't think we should play Las Vegas. "Fellas," I would say patiently, "I just don't think our audience is in Las Vegas."

"Oh, sure they are," said my colleagues. "People come from all over the world to Vegas, and they'll love the show, you'll see!"

Then Sam would move in with the clincher, smiling his amiable smile and waving a sheaf of papers. "Besides," he would say, "this is a wonderful offer from the MGM Grand!"

I seemed to be standing alone in my viewpoint, and finally the combined pleas wore me down. "All right, folks," I said, "if you all really want to do this—we'll do it."

Traditionally we had opened at Harrah's every year with our new show and then taken it on the road. Now we would do the same thing, only open at the Grand. Everybody had grandiose ideas. Jim Hobson wanted to fly an airplane into the Celebrity Room to open the show—at least, I think that's what he had in mind. I didn't quite understand it! And everybody had ideas about what songs they wanted to sing or what the theme of the show should be. Finally, we decided to do a tribute to the great MGM musicals of the past.

We were scheduled to open early in August and Fern and I flew up a couple of days early to get settled. It was terribly hot—August in Las Vegas hovers around one hundred and fourteen degrees—and I was grateful for the air-conditioned mansion MGM had provided for us. I think it was the most sumptuous place Fern and I have ever been in in our lives! It was so large I practically got lost on my way from the kitchen to the bedroom. The living room must have been sixty feet long, with custom-made sofas running the full length of the walls, a grand piano in one corner, and a gilt and crystal coffee table big enough to skate on. We could have put our whole Musical Family in that living room! I was also grateful for the air-conditioned car that MGM put at our disposal. The only time we really suffered from the heat was the few minutes it took for the car to cool off as we backed it out of the garage. MGM took wonderful care of us in every way.

The house was at the edge of a golf course, and around dawn every morning the temperature dropped into the eighties and it was cool enough to play about nine holes of golf, which I did on several occasions. Matty Rosenhaus and his wife and children came out for a few days toward the end of our engagement, and he and I played a short course on a few of those mornings. Looking back, I am so deeply grateful that we had those few days together. It was the last time I ever saw Matty.

Since the time we appeared in Las Vegas, the MGM has suffered its tragic fire, but when we were there, we opened in the Celebrity Room, which seated fourteen hundred people and was one of the largest showrooms in the city. We rehearsed for two days in that cavernous room before we opened, and from time to time I would hike to the back to be sure I could see and hear everything. Each time I did, my heart swelled with pride at how fine my "kids" looked and how well they were putting the show together.

Opening night, Fern got all dressed up in a lovely white gown trimmed in sequins, and Larry and his two little boys, Lawrence Welk the Third and young Kevin, got all dressed up in their three-piece suits and sat with her in her front-and-center booth. Some of our dearest friends were in the room, too, and everyone in the audience seemed to love the show. They gave us a standing ovation when we came out, and a standing ovation at the end, and when the hotel hosted a press reception for us in the penthouse suite, we were told over and over again by some twenty critics and columnists how much they loved the show. We all felt we were off to a rousing start.

But that night something happened which hasn't happened to me in over forty years.

When I walked out on stage for the midnight performance, I faced a room that was only half full. We've been so spoiled by SRO houses everywhere we play, plus an eighteen-month wait for tickets for our TV show in Hollywood, that the sight of that partially filled room really stunned me.

But if I was shocked, it was the "kids" who were really upset—not so much for themselves, as it turned out, but because they were afraid *I* would be unhappy. Their concern really touched me. The little Aldridge sisters rushed up to me after the show, and so did the Otwell twins, and many of the others, all expressing their sympathy and their conviction that everything would be all right the following day. "Wait till the reviews come out," they said hopefully. "Then the room will be jammed!"

But I didn't share their optimism. I've been in the business too long, and gauged audiences for too many years, and I knew that my original assessment was right. Our audience simply was not in Las Vegas. Our audiences are in the communities where families and family life are paramount, and even though we got universally fine reviews, I knew they wouldn't help. We had failed to

123

take something very important into consideration. On tour we generally play in major cities which are surrounded by the smaller towns and cities where many of our fans live; they think nothing of driving one or two or three hundred miles—or more—to come see us. But there are no towns or villages around Las Vegas! Instead, it is surrounded by miles and miles of sand with no cities of any size in any direction. So it was no wonder our audiences were not in Las Vegas. They were waiting for us in their own hometowns.

I tried to explain this to the kids. "It's not that we're not doing a good show, or you're not doing a fine job individually," I told them. "It's just that we are in the wrong place with our type of entertainment."

I honestly didn't feel too bad, and of course I may be overdramatizing the whole thing, because we always had fine houses for the dinner show—it was only the midnight show that fell down.

And in a way I felt the experience was good for us, especially for our younger members. Most of them joined us long after we had become an established show, and they had never experienced the rejection and terrific disappointments—never had to fight for audiences the way we had to in our years and years on the road. I've felt all my life, and still do, that it's the hardships and setbacks that build your character and determine your staying power. So in a way I felt almost grateful on behalf of the younger kids.

But apparently I was the only one who did! Everyone else seemed upset, Sam in particular. One day when he was sighing mournfully, I said, "Sam—this is nothing! When I was with George T. Kelly, we played a show in a town near Enid, Oklahoma, when only one lady came to see us. One! We went out and tried to give her her money back so we wouldn't have to do the show, but it turned out she owned the place and was in on a pass anyway! Compared to that, this is nothing."

Maybe that's one of the rewards of growing older. You can always remember something just as bad—or worse!

I think we develop an ability to see things in their proper perspective as we get along in years. If my orchestra and singers hadn't put forth every effort to do a good show, then yes, I would have been deeply upset. But that wasn't the case at all. It was simply a case of being in the wrong place at the wrong time with our kind of entertainment, and if a few raindrops fell on our heads as a result—well, that wasn't so bad. All we had to do to get out of the rain was go back to our own loyal audience.

And that's exactly what we did.

10. The Best Birthday Present

I'm amazed that I get so much mileage out of my birthday. I think I must have the biggest and longest-lasting party in the world! It not only includes family and friends and fans, it lasts from January to March, and I think you'll agree—that's a long party!

My birthday is actually March 11, but because we tape all our shows six weeks in advance, my kids begin the celebration by "surprising" me with a birthday cake during one of the shows in January. Then Bob Warren, our wonderful, stable announcer, picks up the tempo by telling every studio audience for the next six weeks that my birthday is approaching—and why don't they surprise me by singing "Happy Birthday" when I walk out? Bob looks forward to this occasion all year long because he gets a chance to lead the singing. And while he may be a fine announcer, one of the best in the business—a singer he ain't! Nevertheless, I appreciate the thought and it's really a lovely gesture on the part of Bob and the studio audience to keep my spirits up in the face of yet another birthday.

Then about the first of March, things really move into high gear. That's when we traditionally travel across the country on our spring tour, and from California to Florida and back again, our wonderful audiences sing "Happy Birthday," bring me cards, cookies, candies, and so many birthday cakes that every member of my Musical Family comes home with a few extra pounds. Including me!

I love to go on tour. Performing in front of a live audience is the greatest tonic in the world for me. I remember telling a friend one time that it's actually difficult for me to stand in the wings waiting for my entrance. "I can't wait to get out there," I said. "I'm like an old fire horse waiting for the bell."

It's not only the wonderful exhilaration that comes from performing that makes me so eager. It's also because tours are my "school," my postgraduate course in audience relations. A road-show audience is an instant barometer. I can tell by the sound and amount of applause—or lack of it—just what it is an audience likes. A quiet audience just kills me—that's one thing that would keep me awake nights—and if a number doesn't please an audience, out it goes. That happened back in 1969, at the time rock and roll was so popular. When we were planning our road show that season we thought it would be funny if I came out dressed as a hippie, in a long black wig, granny glasses, and a fur jacket, and opened the show by leading the band in a loud rock number. Then, after a couple of bars, I would stop the music, whip off my wig, and say, "Folks, I was only kidding! We're going back to the music we love!"

The wild applause that greeted that announcement made me realize almost instantly that the audience hadn't been at all pleased by the wild rock and roll that had preceded it—and we took that act out very quickly.

Tours are my schooling all right, but there's something else I love about them, and that's the chance I get to see some of my old friends. In almost every city we play, all across the country, someone will knock at my dressing-room door—and there's a familiar and dear face I haven't seen for a while. Our spring tour in March of 1981, across the southern part of the United States, was certainly no exception. On our opening night in Tucson, Arizona, the door opened, and there were Bill and Alice Breck, my longtime, very close friends. Bill is the Dodge dealer in Tucson and was so very helpful to me in the days when Dodge was sponsoring our show. His lovely lady is an exceptionally fine cello player. I was thinking of hiring her, but Alice decided she'd rather have Bill than a chair in the string section!

From Tucson we flew to Dallas for our second show, and that was wonderful, too, like a big family party. Our dancing star, Elaine Niverson, hails from Dallas, and even though you may not know it from my accent, I'm somewhat a Texan, too! Well, not really, but I spent so many years there in the early part of my career, I've always had a soft spot for those friendly, warmhearted people. And did they cheer when Elaine and Bobby Burgess came out for their first number, wearing yellow satin outfits trimmed in black fringe, to do a rousing version of "Big D" (for Dallas). I want to tell you the house just shook with applause! Elaine's proud parents, Dorothy and Ben Colvin, were there along with about one hundred family friends, and they not only threw a party for the cast afterward, but sent me a delicious birthday cake, too. It was quite an evening. Bobby, incidentally, did six numbers in each of our shows, and one of the high spots was the Charleston he choreographed for himself and Elaine, Mary Lou and Jack, and little Sheila Aldridge and her partner, Michael Redman. All of them were costumed in twenties' flapper outfits, while Bob Ralston—done up in a striped vest, derby hat, and garters on his sleeves— accompanied them on a rinky-dink piano. Suddenly, however, in the middle of the number, Bob would appear to get carried away by the rhythm, leap from his piano bench, and start doing the wildest, longest-legged, highest-kicking Charleston you've ever seen! The audience always screamed with delight with this unexpected surprise, and it was one of the real hits of the show. I myself was astonished the first time I saw Bob dance. Then I found out he and Bobby Burgess had gone to the same dancing school as youngsters, and that Bob

(Ralston, that is) had won the Los Angeles Charleston championship as a boy. What a small world!

From Dallas we flew to Knoxville, where we performed in the Stokely Athletic Center at the University of Tennessee. The nice ladies of the college had prepared a most magnificent buffet for us—ham, roast beef, turkey, wonderful salads and desserts, just beautiful. No wonder southern hospitality is so legendary. It is truly wonderful. Knoxville is the home of four of our stars —Ava Barber, Sheila and Sherry Aldridge, and Jim Turner, and all four of them used every spare moment to visit with their families. Ava and her husband, Roger, not only have their families living there, they have a home of their own. Yes, these two young people have built their very first home, in a woodsy section of town, and they are so proud of it. They live most of the year in Hollywood, of course, working on the show, but come vacation time, they head for Knoxville—and home.

From Knoxville we flew to Gainesville, Florida, then West Palm Beach and then to Lakeland, where my good old friend Walter Windsor from Orlando walked in the door, along with Rusty and Joe Semonski, the parents of the little Semonski girls who used to be on our show. They had a beautiful young lady with them, and at first I didn't recognize her. Then it dawned on me that this was little Michelle, the baby of the group! She had been only nine when the girls first started singing on our show, and it was hard to believe she had grown so much—and so beautifully. Big sister Diane was with them, too, and it was so nice to see them all again. Later, I got Joe Semonski on stage to play accordion so I could have a dance with Mrs. Semonski, who is still one of the best polka dancers I've ever known. Gainesville stands out in my mind for another reason. My old friend Dr. Hugh Allen Bassham bused a group of one hundred and fifty people up from the little town of Whitman—he just about cleared out the whole town! I was so touched at the willingness of people to drive nearly two hundred miles to see my kids perform. That alone was a wonderful birthday present.

From Lakeland we went on to St. Petersburg, and then North Fort Myers, and everywhere we went in Florida it seemed as if everybody was our friend! In fact, Lon Varnell says in another part of this book, it's rare for performers to play more than one concert date in any one area, but in Florida we have so many devoted fans we always have to play extra shows. In this case, we did eight shows in four days. It was exhausting, but satisfying. Many of the folks who come to see us in Florida don't live there—they travel from the North to the warm climate during the cold winter months, and I think some of them must time their vacations so they can be with us. The reception, the warmth, fervent happy birthday wishes, the overwhelming welcome we get from our Florida friends sometimes makes me want to stay there and play forever.

When our concert dates are close together as they are in Florida, it's far more practical and convenient to travel by bus, which is what we did. I enjoy that. There's something about bouncing along together, looking at the beautiful countryside, chatting idly, sometimes singing together in spontaneous and beautiful harmony, that is really fun. Lon always has these bus trips organized flawlessly—so I hope he won't mind if I stop in mid-tour, so to speak, and tell you a little story about one bus trip he would just as soon forget! If he weren't so perfect in everything he does, I wouldn't tell it. But I think it proves that none of us, even someone as perfect as Lon, can go through life without making a little mistake now and then. This happened in Florida six years ago. We had played Lakeland and were due to play St. Petersburg the next day, so next morning I said, "Lon—what time does our bus leave for St. Petersburg?"

"Eleven o'clock, Mr. Welk," said Lon, consulting his schedule. "In fact, you've got time for a little nap before we leave if you like."

Well, since I had been up at five that morning, had a swim and my breakfast, and also because I knew we had two shows to play in St. Petersburg that day, I decided to take him up on it. I went back to bed for a little snooze while he busied himself with the myriad details connected with the tour. At ten-thirty, he knocked on my bedroom door and I got up and dressed while he took our suitcases down to load them onto the bus. Ten seconds later he was back, face pale, eyes bulging, looking as if he were about to faint.

"Oh, Mr. Welk," he gasped, "Mr. Welk—I don't rightly know how to tell you this, but—the bus has left!"

"What!" I cried, astonished. "The bus has left—how could it go without *us?*"

"Well, the schedule said *ten* o'clock, not eleven," said Lon, looking absolutely stricken, "and . . . and the bus driver must have thought we had left early for a press conference in St. Petersburg . . . you know we often do that . . ." Lon stopped, apparently unable to continue, and then he burst out, "Oh, *how* could I have made a mistake like that!"

"Lon," I said, "don't worry about it—we'll get another car."

"Oh, I've already hired a cab, Mr. Welk," he said glumly. "It's waiting downstairs for us."

Sure enough, the cab was waiting, but when the driver discovered we wanted to go to St. Petersburg, he backed out. "Oh, no," he said, putting a hand over his heart. "That's too far, and I'm not a well man. I'll call another cab for you."

He did, and we sat waiting and waiting while Lon grew paler by the minute. Finally another cab pulled up, with a lady driver who said she'd be happy to take us to St. Petersburg for a certain amount of money. Lon immediately agreed, and off we went.

Then we got into a three-way discussion about the shortest route to St. Petersburg. The driver checked with the dispatcher and double-checked with us, and somehow in the middle of the conversation we sailed right by Fourth Street, where we should have turned off, and found ourselves on an eight-mile-long causeway with no hope of getting off till we got to the end and turned around and came back. Sixteen extra miles! Poor Lon. He was aging fast right in front of my eyes, and I really shouldn't have done what I did next . . . but I did! Just to keep things exciting, I peered over the driver's shoulder and murmured, "Oh, dear, it looks like you're getting awful low on gas. You don't think we'll run out of gas, do you?"

"Oh, no!" cried Lon. "No, no, don't tell me that. Don't tell me we're running out of gas. Oh, *please* don't tell me that!"

"We're not running out of gas!" said the driver irritably. "The gas gauge is broke; we have plenty of gas!"

"I'm sorry, Lon," I said, contritely. "I was just putting you on. Now come on, relax. We have plenty of time."

I really wasn't too upset because I knew the first show wasn't scheduled till three o'clock that afternoon, and, unless the whole causeway sunk beneath us, I was reasonably sure we'd make it. But poor Lon was still upset and he fidgeted and fussed till we finally got back on the right road and headed for St. Petersburg. Then he began to relax a little, but he still castigated himself every so often for making such a world-shaking mistake. "Oh, Mr. Welk," he'd say every few miles, shaking his head, "Oh, Mr. Welk, *how* could I have done that!"

Finally, I said, "Lon . . . we've known each other for eleven years, right?"

"Right, yes sir, Mr. Welk, eleven years."

"And in all that time you've never made even one mistake, right?"

"Oh, well, now—I don't know about that, Mr. Welk," he said, thinking hard.

"Well, I do. You haven't. And we're good friends, aren't we?"

"Oh, yes sir, Mr. Welk . . . I . . . you're the dearest, best friend I have in this world."

"Well, then," I said, "don't you think it's about time you stopped calling me 'Mr. Welk' . . . and started calling me 'Lawrence'?"

"Oh," said Lon, "I couldn't do that

—*especially* not now!"

We made the show in plenty of time, and on our spring tour in 1981, Lon was his usual flawless self. We didn't miss any buses, or anything else for that matter, and those five consecutive Florida dates were among the best we've ever played.

From Florida we flew to Biloxi, Mississippi, for the next show and another dose of southern hospitality—more friendly crowds, more happy birthdays and cookies and cakes, and another wonderful surprise. We were staying at the Ramada Inn Airport Hotel near New Orleans, and some friends of Sheila Aldridge—Ethel and Dallas La Salle—sent over seventy-five pounds of that wonderful Louisiana shrimp and crayfish (or "mudbugs," as Sheila calls them!). They wanted to make sure we got a taste of that wonderful Creole cooking. What a feast! I just watched; I didn't eat because my tummy would scream if I did, but the cast loved it. What a nice gesture that was. Pete Fountain's mother was among the guests that night, and she came up on stage and took a bow, and that was nice. And from Biloxi we flew to Austin for the closing night of the tour. My golfing pal Byron Nelson was there, and so was another good friend from my Chicago days—our little Champagne Lady, Jayne Walton. Jaynie came up on stage and I coaxed her into singing "Maria Elena" just as she used to do in the forties. She had a big success with that song in those days, partly because she had been born in Mexico and sang with a perfect Spanish accent. My, how the years rolled away when I heard her sing that song. The audience loved it, too.

And in Austin, Dr. Lee H. Smith, president of South West Texas State University (and Elaine Niverson's uncle), presented me with the biggest birthday cake you've ever seen, a fitting climax to our tour. It was about eight feet by six feet and in the shape of the state of Texas—decorated with cowboy hats and bluebonnets and oil wells, a beautiful cake. Not only that, the university presented all the girls in our cast with bouquets of yellow Texas roses, and when they came out at the close of the first half, wearing pretty blue chiffon gowns and carrying the yellow roses, they made a beautiful, beautiful picture. The warmth, the cake, the flowers, the overwhelming, exploding, spilling, loving applause that engulfed us that night was almost exalting. If only everybody could celebrate their birthday as wonderfully as I am allowed to!

My old pal Elmer Kosub, director of athletics of St. Mary's University, had brought Father James Young, the president, to the show along with Jaynie, and afterward we all drove to the airport in San Antonio, and had dinner there before we boarded our respective planes—Lon to Nashville, and my Musical Family and I to Los Angeles.

In the subdued light of the cabin en route home, I glanced around at my kids—relaxed, now that the tour was over—some chatting softly, others joking and laughing, some snoozing quietly. I was proud of them, so very, very proud! They had behaved perfectly throughout the long and arduous tour—getting up at dawn to make a plane connection, performing eight shows in four days, spending much time traveling from one engagement to the other, and through it all, performing with a spirit and cooperation that made me love them more than ever. They were wonderful! Lon had remarked on their marvelous cooperation, too, just before he left, when he said that our tour had been one of the best, if not the very best in our history. Almost every engagement had been completely sold out,

141

even before we left home. And he said something else that stuck in my mind. He's a specialist in such matters, and he said that in his opinion, the band had played better and the singers performed more perfectly than ever before. "You've reached a new high this year, Mr. Welk," he said.

Now, flying home through the night, I thought, What if I had retired years ago? What if we had missed finding the little Aldridges and the Otwell twins and Anacani and Tom Netherton and Joey Schmidt and all our other fine young talent? What if we had been unable to bring our particular kind of music to our wonderful fans and friends across the nation, fans who depend on us to bring it to them? All of that could have been lost if I had retired, and again I thought that perhaps the experience we accumulate as we travel through life becomes even more valuable as we near the end of our journey, and it's wrong to keep it from being utilized and passed on to others. We should share it. At that moment, flying home in that comfortable, swift plane, with my dear "kids" around me, happy and relaxed, I was very, very glad I hadn't retired.

By the time we landed in Los Angeles at ten-thirty that night, however, I must admit I was good and tired. Fern had gone to Boise, Idaho, to visit our daughter Donna while I was away on tour, but she had returned a day earlier than I and was waiting at home to greet me. It was wonderful to catch up on each other's news and be back home again.

At that point, I would have said my birthday had been more than celebrated. But wait! There's more. I rested for a couple of days, but on Wednesday, March 11, my actual birthday, everything started all over again, a nonstop celebration that began the moment I walked in my office door at seven-thirty in the morning and saw—standing on my desk—a three-foot-high candy band leader, complete with a baton, a big grin, and balloons growing out of his hand! It was one of the most charming little figures I have ever seen, the body made out of foil-wrapped chocolate kisses, with balloon sleeves (one green and one blue), a little cap on his clown face, and "Happy Birthday, Lawrence" printed on one balloon and "from George and Miriam" (Cates) on another. It was just so darling I called everybody in to see it and

that started another round of congrat-
ulations. Then the phone started ringing
and just didn't stop. I would no sooner put
it down than Julie Jobe would press the
buzzer and say, "Here's another one,
Lawrence." At noon my three secretaries,
Laurie, Margaret, and Barbara, stopped the
calls long enough to take me by the hand
and lead me down to the street to a nice
restaurant for a birthday lunch. They sang
"Happy Birthday" too, but in whispers so
nobody else would hear! I figured if the
other diners heard it, I'd never get back to
work.

Back in the office, gazing at my little
clown again, I continued to answer
congratulatory phone calls till Ted and
Larry walked in the door at three o'clock
and escorted me next door, where the
Tooley Company had put together a little
party in honor of our nearly completed new
building, as well as my birthday. It was fun
and different, celebrating in a partially-
completed structure, and even at this point
we could see how strikingly beautiful it was
going to be. Somebody had spirited my
accordion over to the festivities—so what
could I do? I played. And guess what I
played? You're right. Once again, it was

"Happy Birthday"!

By the time I got home I was nearly birthdayed out. But there were more stacks of cards and letters, more telephone calls. I had missed receiving one particular call about six o'clock that morning and I was a little concerned about it. But that night at six o'clock it finally came through—Maxine Gray, my first girl singer, who hasn't missed a year, was calling to wish me another Happy Birthday. That made it official, and when my daughter Shirley and our granddaughter Lisa came over and shared cake and ice cream with Fern and me, the day was truly complete.

Lounging in bed that night, propped up against the pillows, I went over some of the cards and letters and wires I had received. They came from all over, from every walk of life, from my farming friends, show-business pals, golfing pals, even a few senators—and one wire, in particular, which brought tears to my eyes. It was from Gila Rosenhaus, Matty's widow, and their three little girls, and it ended by saying, "I know if Matty were still with us, he would joyfully celebrate this day with you." For just a moment there on my birthday I was filled with sadness at the loss of my wonderful friend. But then I thanked God for the privilege of having known him.

Now you must be saying—that surely must have been the end of the celebration! Nope. One more to go—perhaps the nicest of all. My son, Larry, shares my birthday. Did you know that? Yes, he was born on March 11th, too. (I don't know just how Fern arranged that—you ladies mystify us men sometimes.) At any rate, Larry and I celebrated our joint birthday at an intimate family dinner party at the Bel Air Club the following Sunday afternoon. Just Fern and me, and Shirley and her husband, Bob, and their children, and Larry and his two little boys. Watching Larry with his two sons, I remembered the day he was born. I had gotten so excited I spent every nickel I had calling everybody I knew and shouting, "Fern and I have a son—a boy—we have a son!"

Now, looking at him sitting across the table from me, laughing warmly at something his mother was saying, hugging his own two little boys, I felt an overwhelming gratitude to Fern for keeping our family together with such great love, such great devotion throughout all these years.

Looking at each of my dear ones in turn, my family, I knew that this was the best birthday gift of all.

11. Freedom

When President Ronald Reagan was elected, I felt a tremendous surge of pride. Not because he was from the same general profession as I, and not because we're in accord on many issues, but because we're neighbors! Yes, we live only about two blocks apart, or we did when he was a Pacific Palisades resident. Like everyone else in our area, I was extremely proud that one of "the neighbors" had made it to the White House.

I have known and respected President Reagan for many years, and we had a nodding-waving acquaintance in our neighborhood, which is ordinarily very quiet. But starting on the day he was elected, the streets began swarming with newspaper reporters, cameramen, sightseers, Secret Service men, and television crews. One TV station even rented the tree across the street from the Reagan garage, so they could install a telephone line for direct communication.

The Secret Service men set up a protective blockade at a point where two streets come together in a Y shape—one street going left to President Reagan's home, the other going right to ours. The first night I came home, I had no trouble passing the checkpoint. But the second night one of the security agents motioned me to the side of the road.

"Just a moment, Mr. Welk," he said, "I'd like to speak with you."

I pulled over to the side of the road and parked, carefully rolling down my window and wondering rather uneasily what I had done. "Yes, officer?" I said, smiling winningly as he approached the car. "Mr. Welk," he said, bending over, "I have an accordion I'd like to sell. It's only six hundred dollars."

I was so relieved I almost bought it, but then I remembered I already had several accordions, so regretfully, I turned him down. But he and I and some of the other agents became so friendly during the next few weeks that on some of those cold

November and December nights I brought them up to the house to get warmed up with some hot coffee. I was impressed with all of them. They were courteous, reasonable, and knew their job.

Often during those weeks—and many times since—I would reflect on what a wonderful country this is! Here a man born in a small Illinois town to a family without wealth or special privileges of any kind can become President. And here a man like myself, born of an immigrant farmer and raised in a sod house where bread and milk were often the main meal, can aspire to great dreams—and accomplish them. I don't mean to classify myself in any way with the President! I only want to point out that in this country someone like myself, born into a family as poor and uneducated as mine, has the same chance as someone born into wealth and privilege. I am grateful for this country every time I look at my Musical Family, every time I spend a few days at our place in Escondido, and lately every time I look at the buildings that comprise Welk Plaza.

I can't quite believe those three large buildings. I've never forgotten the day I tried to get a bank loan to build one small office building for our staff. I got turned down flat—and fast! I told this sad story in my book *This I Believe,* but let me just remind you that when I went to my bank and asked about the possibility of getting a loan, the official looked at me a moment and then said loftily, "Mr. Welk, I'll have to discuss this with the other officials." He disappeared and came back two minutes later to say it would be impossible for the bank to lend me anything. "Nothing?" I asked. "Nothing," he said, with finality. I was disappointed but not really surprised— musicians have never been known for their credit! I took the incident philosophically and later, of course, we were able to secure a loan at another bank and go ahead with our first building at 24th and Wilshire.

Ed Spalding oversaw that project with the help of Ted Lennon, and later—Mr. Spalding having passed on—Ted took over the job of putting together the three buildings that comprise Welk Plaza at the corner of Wilshire Boulevard and Ocean Avenue in Santa Monica.

When I first saw that corner, it was occupied by a filling station and a guest hotel. A few years later we acquired the property and Ted set about creating the first of three buildings, the General Telephone building. Next, with the expert help of his brother Jack, he oversaw construction of the Champagne Towers apartment building, and then—just as I was writing this book—the third and final structure, the Wilshire Palisades office building.

I wish I could tell you how I felt when I first saw the Wilshire Palisades. It was just so beautiful that words failed me. Each floor is recessed slightly back from the floor beneath, so the entire structure looks like a white ship with its prow jutting out to sea. The first time I saw the inside was a good three months before completion, and many of the interior walls were not even up. But Ted was anxious for me to see what progress had been made, so one bright and sunny morning in February—one of those golden California days when the sun is shining brightly and a soft warm wind is blowing and the sea is a glittering sheet of blue, he and I walked over and took the workmen's elevator up to the eighth floor. I might just tell you that a workmen's elevator is not the same as the speedy ones you and I are used to in these new high-rise buildings, at least not the one we used. No—a man in a hard-hat poked a long stick into some kind of electrical connection at the top of the elevator, and then we lumbered up very, very slowly, up, up, up to the eighth floor. When we arrived, the man pushed the doors apart and held them till we got out. I started to joke with him, but when I turned and looked out the windows at the view before us—words failed me. To the south, I could see far down the coastline, past the Santa Monica pier and, in my mind's eye, past the old Lick Pier where the boys and I had played for so many years at the Aragon Ballroom. To the north I could see the same coastline curving into the green and rugged Santa Monica coastal mountains. It was so beautiful I really couldn't say anything. Ted took me by the arm and led me into what would be my office—a large, spacious area overlooking the sea, with sliding glass doors that lead out onto a wide, wide balcony— "Big enough," said Ted, gesturing eagerly, "so you can have a little putting green out here, Lawrence! And some trees and shrubs in big pots."

I still couldn't answer him. The beauty of the place, the way the space was enclosed, the patios and wide balconies on every floor, were just too much for me. Finally I said, "Thousands and thousands of one-night stands." He was startled. "What?" "It took thousands and thousands of one-night stands to get here, Ted," I told him. "And you'll never know how grateful I am."

It's true. It took thousands and thousands of one-nighters, some in freezing weather, some in weather so hot it was like playing in a steam bath. It took a few heartbreaks and a lot of disappointments, as well as some wonderful thrills, and I wouldn't have traded any of it. Not any of it. I wouldn't trade a single day in this wonderful country for a day anywhere else in the world.

I said as much to Ted as we stood on that wide balcony with the sun warming our heads and the breeze rippling the palm trees edging the Palisades beneath us. He nodded. He understood exactly what I meant because he and I are from somewhat the same mold, from families that were poor in material possessions but rich in love; and we both understand what a blessing it is to live in a country where anyone from any background can make his dreams come true, where opportunities still exist—and freedom still lives.

That is our great blessing in this country—freedom—and I realized it as never before, standing there in that warm sunshine. It was freedom that had let me leave a sod house in the middle of a North Dakota prairie and set out to try and make my dreams come true. It was freedom that had let me dare to dream dreams that might have seemed laughable in any other country but ours. It was freedom that had opened doors and cleared pathways and helped me climb to this towering and lovely building. I was filled with a passionate gratitude and I thought: Ours is a country where you don't need special privilege, rank, education, inherited wealth, or even a knowledge of the English language to succeed. All you need is the desire—and the determination to work for your dreams.

12. Hear Ye! . . . Hear Ye!

As I said, Ted and I are somewhat from the same mold. He, too, was born into a religious, hardworking family, and was taught to work from his earliest years. Later, when his father died, young Ted and his brothers supported their mother and the younger children by taking every job they could find. It was hard, of course, very hard, but I'm convinced that the tremendous character and know-how and integrity Ted evidences today are a direct result of the demands made on him when he was growing up.

Ted has done things for us I would never have dreamed of. I never wanted anything in this life except to put together the best band and best entertainment I could. But along came Ted, who opened our eyes to other opportunities, and in the process, he has provided a good living for the hundreds of people who now work in our offices and our resort in Escondido. When I talk about the wonderful people who have come into my life, Ted Lennon is right up there at the top of the list.

And I love his enthusiasm! He always has his eye out for an opportunity, and along that line, I'd like to tell you a little story about him. I just wish you could hear him tell it himself. His Irish sense of humor and drama really make it live.

This all happened along about 1970, as I recall. I had been out playing golf one afternoon, and no sooner walked in the front door of my home than the phone rang. It was Ted. "Boss," he said, without preamble, "how'd you like to gamble twenty-five dollars to get me a little education?"

I laughed. "Twenty-five dollars? What for?"

"Well, that's the plane fare to San Diego. There's an auction going on there at the County Courthouse at eleven o'clock in the morning—a 470-acre parcel of land right next door to our place in Escondido, and if I get to the auction in time, I might be able to pick it up for us at a pretty good price!"

He went on to explain some of the details of the projected transaction, suggesting we limit our initial involvement to something like $115,000, and it may give you some idea of the trust and confidence I have in him, that I broke in and said, "Ted, why don't you just go ahead? If you think this is a good idea, I'm willing to gamble with you."

Ted had heard about the property only a few days earlier when a Realtor had telephoned and told him he had some acreage for sale contiguous to our eastern property line in Escondido. "It could be worth a million dollars," he informed Ted, "but if you want it, you'll have to act fast."

Ted had acted very fast indeed, making phone calls and inquiries and discovering that the property in question was not just up for sale but was being auctioned off at foreclosure proceedings, and furthermore, if the bidding didn't go sky-high, there was a good chance of acquiring it for $114,000 instead of a million! It was at that point that he called me.

There was only one hitch. The sale was scheduled for the next morning, and Ted knew next to nothing about foreclosure

158

sales. "I had a vague romantic picture of a dignitary coming out on the courthouse steps and ringing a bell and shouting . . . "Hear Ye, Hear Ye, this sale is now in session," he confessed. "But I really knew nothing about it and I had no idea how to go about bidding." Concerned, he called our banker and told him the whole story. "Oh," replied the financier, "you've got nothing to worry about. The vice-president of our branch in San Diego used to be in real estate and knows all there is to know about foreclosure sales. He'll be glad to help you." "Great!" said Ted. "Now, I'll need some cash too—any problems there?" "None whatever," said our friend, "you can have whatever you need."

Bright and early the next morning, at six-fifteen to be exact, Ted appeared at my front door with two checks for me to sign —one for a cashier's check and one for forty thousand in cash. I signed them both and Ted left immediately for the Los Angeles Airport and the seven-thirty flight to San Diego. Aboard the plane, he went over his schedule. First, he would go to the title and trust office and get a full description of the property ("I didn't want to buy a pig in a poke," he told me later).

Then to the bank to pick up instructions and the necessary money, and finally to the sale itself at eleven o'clock. It was tight, but barring some unforeseen complication, Ted felt he would make it.

But almost immediately Fate stepped in and began to rearrange his schedule! His plane arrived in San Diego on time, but just as it came in for a landing, a small plane darted in beneath it, forcing it to veer off and circle the field again before coming in for another landing. The whole incident probably took only twenty minutes or so, but it was enough to make Ted a little edgy, and when the plane finally landed and taxied up to the terminal, he raced through the lobby and out the front door, coattails flying, briefcase clutched firmly in his hand. Bert Carter, our manager in Escondido, was waiting for him, and the two men drove swiftly over to the title office to get a description of the property.

But the clerk refused to give it to him. "But, ma'am!" cried Ted. "That property is being auctioned off at eleven o'clock this morning! How can I bid on it if I don't know anything about it?"

"I'm sorry," repeated the clerk, stiffly, "but that information is private, privy only to the beneficiary of the trust and the lawyers involved. I cannot give it to you.''

Ted heaved a frustrated sigh, but of course there was nothing he could do about it, so he and Bert drove over to the bank. It was nine-thirty-five by Ted's watch as they pulled up in front of the bank. "Why don't you just park in that twenty-minute zone and wait for me there, Bert?'' he suggested. "This should take only a few minutes.''

Inside the bank, the banker was waiting, as promised. "Good morning, Mr. Lennon,'' he smiled, ushering Ted into his private office. "Now, what can I do for you?''

"Well,'' said Ted, "if you'll be good enough to tell me just how I go about bidding at this foreclosure sale and what kind of money I should take with me.''

The banker regarded him blankly. "I don't know,'' he said.

"You don't know!'' Ted was startled. "But our man in Los Angeles said you were a former Realtor and knew everything about foreclosure sales!''

"I never handled a foreclosure sale in my life,'' said the banker firmly.

Ted opened his mouth to protest, thought better of it, and closed it again. "Well, okay," he muttered, "I . . . I guess I'll just *guess* what I have to do. Here . . ." he slid the two checks I had signed across the desk. "Then if you'll just give me a cashier's check for seventy-five thousand dollars, and forty thousand in cash."

The banker cleared his throat. "Well," he said, "the cashier's check is no problem. But—I can't give you the cash."

"Can't give me the cash!" Now Ted's jaw really did drop. "You mean to tell me you don't have forty thousand dollars in the bank?"

"Yes, of course we do," replied the banker a little testily. "But the bank vault doesn't open till quarter to eleven."

"You're kidding," said Ted, unbelieving. "You're kidding! The sale starts at eleven o'clock, and if I'm not there with the cash, I'll lose our chance to bid!"

"Well, let's see what I can do," murmured the banker, and he began making a series of phone calls while Ted alternately paced the floor, looked at the clock on the wall, and tried to stay calm. Fifteen minutes went by. Five more. At ten-twenty-five the banker hung up the phone, jumped up, said, "Wait here, I'll be right back," and strode out the door. Another ten minutes passed. Five more. At ten-forty-one Ted sighed, convinced his chance to bid at the sale had passed irretrievably, when suddenly the banker rushed back into the room. "Here's your forty thousand," he said, quickly handing Ted a stack of five-thousand-dollar packets held together with rubber bands. Ted jammed them into his briefcase along with the cashier's check, zipped the case shut and locked it ("I did everything but chain it to my wrist!" he told me later), and rushed out the door. The banker rushed right along behind him, telling Ted he had also located a young lady in the escrow department who used to work in real estate. "And," he added, triumphantly, "she is very knowledgeable about foreclosure sales!"

"Wonderful," said Ted, running across the lobby with his briefcase. "Ask her if she can meet me there, will you? She can let me know how the bidding is going."

"I will," said the banker breathlessly, "and I'll come, too. I want to find out how these things are done myself!"

It was exactly twelve minutes to eleven by the big clock on the wall of the bank lobby as Ted dashed out the front door to meet Bert. But Bert had gotten nervous in the meantime, waiting in the twenty-minute zone, moved the car to another parking spot, and was now inside the bank looking for Ted! So there was Ted outside the bank looking for Bert, while Bert was inside looking for him, as the precious minutes ticked inexorably away. Ted was about to jog over on his own when he finally spotted Bert. They jumped in the car and careened madly over to the county courthouse which, fortunately for everyone concerned, was only a few blocks away, and as Bert slid into a parking space, Ted jumped out and began running across the green lawns toward the courthouse. "And I give you my word of honor," says Ted in almost reverential tones as he recalls that incident, "I give you my word of honor that just as I reached the bottom step the door at the top opened and out came the auctioneer, ready to begin the sale. We had made it!"

Then the dramatic process of the sale itself began. There stood the auctioneer on the steps, just as Ted had pictured it. But what he hadn't pictured was the large and interested crowd of onlookers—the usual courthouse collection of retired businessmen and hangers-on, plus a few derelicts and winos, a couple of whom were stretched out on the lawn snoring loudly. Ted clutched his briefcase tightly, mindful of the forty thousand dollars inside, as the auctioneer intoned: "This foreclosure sale is now in session. Will the bidders step forward and be recognized, register their names with me, and show me their wherewithal?"

Ted stepped forward, registered his name, and showed his cashier's check to the auctioneer. He peered at it closely and then nodded. Ted was permitted to bid.

Next, two gentlemen who turned out to be the owners of the second trust deed made themselves known to the auctioneer and were duly recognized. "Does anyone else wish to bid?" asked the auctioneer, gazing slowly around the group, which for the most part looked as if it couldn't bid on a cup of coffee, except for one man leaning up against a tree, smoking a big black cigar. The auctioneer waited expectantly, but when the man continued to stand silently, puffing away on his cigar, the auctioneer turned back to the crowd and said, "Let the bidding begin!"

Ted looked around the crowd, and when nobody said anything, decided to open the bidding himself with a bid one thousand dollars lower than the amount of the second trust deed. Taking a deep breath, he said loudly: "Seventy-three thousand dollars!"

The two gentlemen who held the trust deed made an immediate counterbid: "Seventy-four thousand!"

"Seventy-*five* thousand," said Ted firmly.

Another pause, while everyone in the group turned with interest to the two gentlemen. They conferred as the minutes ticked by, and Ted began to hope they would bow out. But no . . . "Seventy-five thousand *one hundred* dollars!" came their bid, loud and clear.

"Aha!" thought Ted, two can play at that game, and he came back immediately with "Seventy-five thousand *two* hundred dollars!"

"Just a minute," said the auctioneer to Ted. "I have to see your money."

"But I've already shown you my cashier's check, sir," said Ted.

"Yes, but I have to see if you have the wherewithal to support this new bidding."

"Uh . . . well, I do have it, sir," said Ted, only too aware of the forty thousand in cash nestled inside his briefcase.

"I have to *see* it," repeated the auctioneer inexorably.

At this time, the banker stepped forward. "I'm the vice-president of his bank," he said importantly, "and I will personally guarantee he has the money."

"I don't care who you are," said the auctioneer, "I have to see it."

Ted looked again at the crowd, which now seemed to his fevered eye to be moving in a little, and he said, "Uh . . . could we go over there in the corner, please?" The auctioneer nodded. "Very well." He and Ted retreated about twenty feet away to a corner of the building, where Ted carefully unlocked the briefcase, unzipped it, and opened it just wide enough so the auctioneer could peer inside.

"Migawsh!" said the auctioneer . . . or words to that effect. "I'll be darned, you *do* have it, don't you! Say, how much you got in there?"

"There are five thousand dollars in each of those packets," said Ted in a stage whisper, "and I've got eight of them."

"Well, that's good enough for me," said the auctioneer. "I assume you'll stop bidding if the sale goes above that amount?"

"Right," said Ted, zipping the case shut and cradling it back in his arms.

The auctioneer remounted the steps. "The bid is now seventy-five thousand two hundred dollars," he intoned. "Any further bids?"

"Seventy-five thousand *three* hundred," said the two gentlemen quickly. Ted gulped. Now the waters were getting a little deeper. "Going," said the auctioneer, "going . . ."

"Seventy-five thousand *four* hundred dollars," cried Ted, interrupting the auctioneer.

"Seventy-five thousand *four* hundred dollars," repeated the auctioneer. "The bid is now seventy-five thousand four hundred dollars . . . . Going *once* . . . going *twice* . . ." (he looked over at the two gentlemen, who stood silently) "Sold! . . . to Mr. Ted Lennon, for seventy-five thousand four hundred dollars!"

Elated, Ted began to follow the auctioneer inside the courthouse, where the final details of the sale would be concluded. As he did, the man with the cigar disengaged himself from the crowd and said to Ted, "I got you a pretty good bargain, didn't I?"

"How's that again?" said Ted.

"I got you a pretty good bargain," repeated the man. "I'm the one who called you about this piece of property in the first place!''

"Oooooh, yes!" said Ted. "Well, I *do* thank you—for a wonderful tip!"

Thanks to Ted's shrewdness and his fast acquisition of foreclosure facts, we were able to acquire a piece of property which has become extremely valuable in the intervening years. In fact, for twenty-five dollars, I would say it was one of the most successful investments we've ever made.

No, on second thought, I think maybe the best investment I ever made was hiring Ted Lennon!

13. Friendship: From A to Z

Talking about friends I meet on tour reminds me of how very important friendships are in life. I think that's especially true as we get on in years. Without good friends, life could surely become very, very dull, and I think we need to make new friends all through life. I've been fortunate in that I've always had a lot of friends, partly, I suppose, because I truly like people. Whenever I find someone I respect and admire, I try to keep them a friend for life. I have friends dating back to my farm years in Strasburg, and that's a long time ago! In fact, I try to fly "home" every spring to renew old ties with my family and friends, such as my golfing pal Buster Hogue, whose friendship has meant so much to me over the years. And I still correspond with some of the musicians from our first little bands who traveled on the road with me, a whole spectrum of show-business friends, as well as longtime personal friends of Fern and myself. All my friendships are extremely valuable to me, but there does seem to be a special warmth to those that go back a few years. If you and I are old friends, chances are we remember the same things, share the same memories, recall the slogans and dances and customs that youngsters of today have never even heard about. It's a great bond, and I cherish the friends of my youth and middle years. But I also cherish my young friends of today. They bring a freshness and sparkle and happy optimism to everything we do, and I love to be around them. That includes very young children. My friends tell me that whenever I'm entertaining in the restaurant in Escondido and I spot a little baby, it's the baby who ends up in my arms instead of the accordion! Chances are the little one and I will then have a dance for ourselves while Joey Schmidt takes over on the accordion.

The truth is, I love people, and if you asked me who my best friends were, I'd have a little trouble answering you. But I must admit that among those closest to my

171

heart are the ones I've often threatened to adopt—my musical children, my "kids," the members of my Musical Family. They're not only my coworkers, they're my very dear friends. And I'd like to tell them—and you—how very much they mean to me, right now.

From A to Z

I've talked about my Musical Family from time to time in some of my books, but this time I thought I'd go right down our membership roster, from A to Z, and tell you why I love and respect each one of them, and how much their affection and loyalty have added to my life. You may notice, as I go through this long list of names, that the great majority have been with me for years—some over thirty. (My secretary Laurie Rector complains that I'm always asking her in front of others how long she has been with me. "Twenty-five and a half years," she answers reluctantly, and then mutters, "Now everybody is adding up and saying "twenty-five *years!* Gosh, she must be at least umpty years old!'")

But I never think of my "kids" as getting old, not even the ones who have been with me over thirty years, like Barney Liddell and Myron Floren and Dick Dale and Curt Ramsey—and of course my sensational first secretary, Lois Lamont, who joined me back in 1945. (Now you folks can start figuring out how old Lois is!)

The first names—under *A*—are the little Aldridge sisters, and I bless the day these talented girls came into my life. I was convinced we didn't need any more singers when they first auditioned for me, but they were equally convinced we did! And after you folks got a look at them when they made their first appearance on the show, you were convinced, too. Sheila is the smaller of the two; Sherry is the blonde who often sings the high, sweet obbligato during their numbers with the Otwell twins. Both these southern beauties (they're from Knoxville, Tennessee) are married now— Sheila to Roger Behr of the well-known comedy team of Roger and Roger; and Sherry to Bob Davis, our wonderful flute player—I guess that makes Sherry and Bob a real musical "family." It has been our honor and pleasure to have Bob in our reed section since 1966, and the girls since 1977. Both Sheila and Sherry agree that having husbands in the same general profession is a real plus. "We love our work," says Sherry, "and Bob and I have so much in common, being in the orchestra together." I might tell you that Sheila and her husband, Roger Behr, have a darling little four-pound white "teacup" poodle as their family pet. The doggie's name is Andy-Bear. "So," says Sheila with a twinkle, "naturally that makes us The Three Behrs!" Well, I don't know about that. I do know it is wonderful having these three talented and dedicated people in our Musical Family.

Next on our list, under *B,* is Bob Ballard, our arranger. You folks don't see much of him, but we all value him so very, very highly, not only for his musical expertise in arranging our music and directing our choral groups, but for his unflappable, genuine serenity. Bob, who has been with us since 1974, is my definition of a true gentleman and a great talent. Bob—I salute you!

Next, Ava Barber, our popular "country gal." I've often told the story of how

Ava followed me around the golf course in Nashville in 1974 while her husband, Roger, played a tape recording of her voice. I was amused and charmed by their ingenuity, and by Ava's talent, and as the years go by I have become completely sold on her as a performer and a person. I may be a little prejudiced, but I think Ava just gets prettier every year. (I might just take this opportunity to tell you that Ava's husband, Roger Sullivan, is a jewel on our tours. He helps Jack Imel and Barney Liddell so much we couldn't do without him.) Ava is my definition of a truly lovely lady—kind, loving, goodhearted in every way.

Now here we are with Bobby Burgess. What a talent! He always comes through with something entertaining and just a little different. Bob has had three partners on our show, starting with Barbara Boylan in 1961, then Cissy King, and now Elaine Niverson. Dark-eyed Elaine had a tough act to follow when she joined Bobby in 1978. This lovely lady not only had to jump into Cissy's shoes and learn a myriad of new dance routines, she also had to find her own place in our viewers' affections. She went right to work, rehearsing new numbers for hours and hours every day—tap, tango, rhumba, adagio, waltz, polka—a new and different number every week. It wasn't long before her bright smile and obvious talent had made her a solid favorite with our viewers, and she and Bobby have now become one of our most popular acts. Oh, I must tell you a cute story about Bobby. Did you know he was a birthday present recently? Well, he was, even if he didn't come tied up in a red ribbon. It seems that a lady named Sally Zaun celebrated a most important birthday a few months ago, and although she liked the gift her husband gave her, she informed him later that what she had really wanted was a dance with Bobby Burgess. Well, Mr. Zaun isn't a loving husband for nothing. A month later he threw a party at the Thunderbird Country Club in Palm Springs, where the Zauns live, and unbeknownst to his wife, hired Bobby to fly down and surprise her. When he cut in on the unsuspecting Mrs. Zaun as she was waltzing around the floor, and she looked up to see who her new partner was, her shock and delight were more than worth the trip. I'm not surprised that Bobby was willing to do that. He's one of the nicest people I've ever known, and he and his wife, Kristie, and their two lovely babies, Becki and Robert, are a wonderful, completely devoted little family. I'm proud to count them as my friends.

Now we get to the *C's*—and George Cates. Well—I could write a whole book about this gentleman, and I think I will right now!

George is not the gentle, diplomatic type. No, he's more like Mt. Vesuvius, sending up sparks of fire, blowing up regularly, and generally holding everybody's strict attention! When he first joined us in 1951, some of the boys didn't exactly care for his high-voltage personality, but when they discovered he had a tremendous sense of humor as well as a phenomenal command of his profession, the battle was over and George had the troops firmly in command.

He suffered a massive heart attack just a few months after I first hired him, back in 1951, when we were playing at the Aragon in Santa Monica. We kept him in the family, however, because I was convinced he would be a tremendous asset to us, and time has certainly proven me right. I believe George has developed—and I hope you'll agree with me—the finest orchestra in the nation today.

He's a workaholic, just like me. Last year he was stricken with a severe eye problem right in the middle of rehearsal. He was rushed off to the hospital for delicate and crucial eye surgery that very evening. We all expected he would have a long convalescence, but two weeks later he was back on stage, waving his arms, raising his voice, making beautiful music, and generally being George.

He and his beautiful wife, Miriam, have added much to my life with their warm and understanding friendship, and I shall never stop thanking God for sending this driving, persistent, brilliant, and altogether wonderful man into my life. George—I salute you. These years with you have been wonderful.

Next on the *C*'s is Henry Cuesta. There are a lot of reasons I like Henry. He's not only a brilliant clarinetist and a great asset to our show, but his wife, Janette, makes the best lemon sponge cake in the world! Occasionally Henry brings one of Janette's cakes to rehearsal. If it arrives at the studio without a few bites missing, we're doing very well, but it rarely lasts through the morning.

Somehow people find an excuse for coming in to "visit" me, and naturally I have to say, "Would you like a piece of this cake?" and naturally they say "Would I"—and there it goes. Henry has been with us since he left his starring spot leading a jazz group at the Skyline Hotel in Toronto, Canada, in 1972, and am I glad! He and his lovely Janette and their three children are an exceptionally close and loving family, and I just love to spend time with them.

D is for Dick Dale. Looking at Dick, it's hard for me to believe he joined us in Chicago over thirty years ago! To me, he still looks like a college student—well, maybe a postgraduate. Dick is one of our more versatile performers. He sings, dances, plays beautiful sax tones—and also plays Santa Claus on our Christmas show. There now, I've given away the secret!

Dick makes a super Santa, but he tells me that every year it seems there are more and more children, and Santa has to run around handing out more and more presents. Last year, as he jogged past me delivering yet another gift, he panted, "Santa is getting too old for this job!" Dick—just stay as young as you are.

Next under the *D*'s is Ken Delo, who came to us from Detroit via Australia, where he was one of their leading TV stars. He has built an enormous following over the years. Ken has that something extra—a quick wit, an eye for the absurd, a way of singing directly to our audience. Whenever we have a novelty or nonsense number, Ken gets it. And yet, I don't know if you folks remember him sitting on a stool and singing "Beautiful Girls Walk a Little Slower" on one of our recent shows, but it was one of the warmest, most sensitive and moving renditions I've ever heard. Ken and his lovely wife, Marilyn, have two darling children, and I'm so happy he joined us in 1969.

Arthur Duncan. If there's a nicer person in our band, I don't know who it is. Arthur was one of twelve children, so maybe he was already conditioned to getting along with others when he joined us in 1964. He was already a major star in Europe when he came back to Los Angeles and danced for me at the Palladium one afternoon during a band rehearsal. I was so taken with those nimble dancing feet and happy smile, I knew we had to have him on the show. Arthur's an expert in the field of tap dancing, of course, but somehow it's his genuine niceness that has made him so very, very popular with everyone—including me!

Well, here we are to the *E's*—and the very first name on the list I can't pronounce! Anacani Echeverria—that's a mouthful for such a beautiful little lady. I don't think I'm exaggerating when I say she is just as beautiful on the inside as she is on the outside. Anacani encountered a certain amount of resistance when she first joined us in 1972. I'm not sure what it was, maybe a little jealousy of her natural beauty and delicate voice. But her own innate niceness and charm soon won everybody over. She's always been pretty, but since her marriage to her handsome young lawyer-husband, Rudolfo Echeverria, in 1978, she's blossomed into an authentic beauty. Recently she won a role in the movie, *Zoot suit,* a tale of life in the Mexican community in Los Angeles. We were all pleased that she had a chance to try something new in her career, but we missed her during the six weeks she was filming her part—and so did our fans, judging by the letters we received. I have always felt that Anacani had much to do with the success of Escondido. She was our first Singing Hostess there, you may recall, and she became such a favorite with everyone that people used to come just to see her. She quite literally walked into my life! I was walking out the door of our Escondido restaurant just as she was walking in—and I've been grateful ever since. A lovely, lovely lady.

Ernie Ehrhardt, who plays cello, has one of the most beautiful tones I've ever heard, and no wonder. In addition to his own fine technique, he plays a cello over two hundred years old, an authentic Gagliano, signed in 1760. I'm always deeply touched and pleased when I see how the men in our band make every effort to acquire the finest possible instruments. How lucky I am to have such dedicated musicians! A Los Angeles native, Ernie played with both the Los Angeles Philharmonic and Houston Symphony before joining us in 1972.

Now we're up to *F,* and Gail Farrell. You'll find the full story of Gail, Ron, and Michael elsewhere in this book, but once again I'd like to say that she has made probably the greatest personal development of anyone I've ever had in the band.

And here's Joe Feeney. Ah, me—again, I could write another book! I'll restrain myself and just say that Joe has been with me since 1957, when he moved out here from Grand Island, Nebraska. He added to our Musical Family—and he promptly began adding to his own! He and his wife, Georgia, now have nine little Feeneys, three of them still at home. Joe has the kind of vocal equipment that comes along only rarely, and when he lets go with one of his fine Irish songs, he can—and does—move our audience to cheers and tears. I like to take Joe with me to dinner parties and informal concerts where he can sing directly to the ladies. He's always a great hit—and I get a chance to play accompaniment!

Myron Floren. Myron has written his own book, *The Accordion Man,* and I hope you'll read it because his life story is a real inspiration. Myron has added so much to all our lives! He's been an invaluable help to me, of course, assisting with conducting the band and taking over many, many duties whenever we go on tour. I always feel I can depend on Myron completely, no matter what we ask of him.

In a little foreword I wrote for his book, I said he's so self-controlled that at times he doesn't seem human! Well, of course he is—in fact, he's really very emotional. But what I meant was that he always behaves with total dignity and kindness, no matter what the pressures. It just amazes me. Myron is a truly wonderful man. I would say that every one of us in the band really loves him, and we're lucky to have him.

G for Sandi Griffiths, our lovely red-headed mother of five—young Daniel Jensen Griffiths arrived on May 3, 1981, to join his three big sisters and one brother. Sandi has been on a leave of absence while she cares for her young and growing family. But her warm smile and beautiful personality will always be a part of our Musical Family.

Next are the *H*'s, and Bob Havens! Bob has been our slide-trombone man since 1960 and if you want to see a happy Welk, just watch my face—or feet—when Bob is blowing some of his wonderful riffs. He's a genius at what he does, and everybody in the band agrees he's one of the finest jazzmen in the United States, if not the world. George Thow says that Bob can play a four-octave run, "which is impossible —only Bob doesn't know that!" How fortunate we are to have him.

Laroon Holt. Laroon Holt was a child prodigy, and his beautiful, dependable playing in our trumpet section has been a joy since 1973. It looks as though talent runs in the family, because Laroon's pretty fifteen-year-old daughter, Heidi, is a wonderful pianist, with great natural style—perhaps you saw her on our Christmas show. It appears to me she has a real chance to go places in the music business.

Larry Hooper. Our dear Larry Hooper is on an extended leave of absence, due to ill health. If you've read any of my other books, you know what a brave and stalwart man he is, never complaining, always optimistic, always working toward the day he can be with us again. I guess Larry is most famous for singing "Oh, Happy Day" in that deep bass voice of his. Larry—it will be a happy day for all of us, fans and Musical Family members alike, when you come back to us.

Next are Guy and Ralna Hovis. Guy and Ralna are two of the most talented people who ever walked through the front door of my office to audition for me. One of our talent scouts found Ralna for us—but it was Ralna who found Guy! "My husband has a wonderful voice," she told us. "Please listen to him." We did, she was right, and when we put the two of them on the air together, their very first appearance drew such tremendous fan response we knew we had found a pair of winners.

Since their lovely little daughter, Julie Miranda, arrived to join them about four years ago, Ralna has concentrated more and more on being a mama, and doesn't sing with us quite as often. But Guy continues to brighten the show with his unique voice and styling every week. I'm just grateful with all my heart that these two extremely talented, sensitive, and very special people came into my life when they did. They have added to it immeasurably.

Paul Humphrey. Paul Humphrey joined us

186

in 1975. I was delighted to get him because he is widely regarded as one of the best drummers in the business. Paul has two of the cutest children you've ever seen, and I know you'll agree with me if you've seen them on our Christmas shows. Daughter Pier is a fine little dancer; and young Damien, age two, plays drums with one big eye on his daddy to see if he's doing okay! Looks like he's destined for the music world, too.

Harry Hyams, as befits the gentleman he is, sits quietly in the back row in the string section, doing nothing but playing perfect viola tones and adding great depth and richness to our band. I've always been grateful that this fine musician joined our band in 1961. He's sought after by symphony orchestras and other bands all the time, but he stays loyal to us.

And now—Skeets Herfurt! I found Skeets all by myself. I'd heard about him for years, but he was always busy playing with bands like Tommy Dorsey and Glenn Miller. Then when I heard he had retired in 1978, I tracked him down to La Jolla, California, and talked him into coming with us. He tells a little story you may have heard—about how I replaced him and his little college band at Eddie Ott's Broadmoor Club in Denver, Colorado, back in the twenties, and it took him fifty years to catch up with our band. Today, watching Skeets play with such effortless technique and beauty, I can only say: "Skeets—what took you so long?"

And here's our wonderful producer, Jim Hobson. Another man who deserves a book. I don't know what it is about Jim—he does more than anyone else to create and produce our show, but somehow everyone gets credited but him. And yet he's the key to our show. I think we've come to expect such perfection from him during the last twenty-six years that we tend to take it as a matter of course. I would like to go on record right now as saying Jim is, without question, the best director and producer of a musical show in the history of the business. I know of no one else who could take fifty different talents, mold them, rehearse them, direct them—and have them tape an entire hour show in just one day. It's just not done by any other show—we're the last of the breed—and it's

188

due in very large part to Jim.

Whatever differences Jim and I have had over the years are due entirely to his creative genius and drive to do something different in the way of production each week. I'm more pragmatic (didn't know I knew that word, did you?) and I want to go along with what I know, from experience, will please our audience the most. Jim wants to experiment, and you can't blame him for that. His mind awes me. He constantly comes up with ideas that are really out of this world. If he had his way, we'd have overhead cameras and volcanoes spouting lava, and streams built across stage so real live boats could sail on them. As a matter of fact, we did that in the early days of our show. Jim Roberts and Norma Zimmer went sailing across stage in a canoe on a man-made stream, and halfway across the canoe tipped over and dunked them both in the water!

Our Musical Family has grown to the point now, however, where we can't accommodate such lavish production numbers very often. Instead, we've become more of a family gathering, during which everyone tries to get into the act. I tend to concentrate more on the personality and individuality of each singer, while Jim, with his brilliant theatricality and overall eye for television, tends to see things in dazzling production numbers. He started out in life to be an actor, and I imagine he would have been a great one, with his flair for dramatics.

Jim works long, hard hours—his office is really in his head, and no matter where he is, his mind is always on the show. I don't know of anyone I respect, admire, or love more than this bundle of genius and talent. Jim—from the heart, I thank you for what you have done for me—and the show.

There's only one *I* in the band and it's Jack Imel. Jack is one of my favorite stories, because he was the original Peck's Bad Boy when we found him, right after World War II. In fact, he was still wearing his sailor suit when he first performed on our show in 1957. Jack had his troubles adjusting to reality! Things like paying bills on time, or even remembering what time it was, sort of confused him till we took drastic steps to help him get organized. When Jack recognized that he was wasting his energies, he made a complete turnaround and all his creative juices went into the show. He has become so valuable that it's thrilling. He helps direct the show and comes up regularly with novelty song-and-dance numbers for himself and Mary Lou, and on tour, he does just about everything! I feel extra proud of Jack because he accomplished so much over so many hurdles. He's become such a help that if I had to get along without Jack—I think I'd throw in the towel!

And now for the *L*'s. You'll notice that Russ Klein has sneaked in here with Lois Lamont. That's okay—they're married! Lois has been my out-of-this-world secretary since 1945, and I don't think the band would be what it is today without her loyal help. She devoted her entire life to us till she fell so seriously ill in 1973. She doesn't do quite as much work now as she used to—her sister, Laurie, has taken over many of her duties, and I must say Laurie does an equally superlative job. She's the one who reminds me of what I have to do next—and that's become a full-time job! Both Laurie and Lois have added so much to my life and I'm deeply grateful to both of them.

I couldn't have been happier when Lois married Russ. He's one of the nicest, kindest men I've ever known, as well as being a superb, totally professional musician. Russ is my "chauffeur" on Tuesdays. He drives five of us to the studio in his big blue Cadillac. I've tried to be loyal to Dodge all these years, but I must admit that driving with Russ in his Caddie makes this "boss" feel as if he's finally made it!

Next under the *L*'s is Neil Levang, another superlative musician. When Barbara Mandrell guested on our show, she was very impressed with Neil and his guitar playing. No wonder—he's a true artist, and I'm not saying that just because he's from North Dakota. Neil's been with us since 1959, and I just want to say, Neil—it's been a pleasure all the way.

Barney Liddell! Notice the exclamation point. Well, that's just how I feel about Barney. He's larger than life, and I don't mean just his size. You can ask Barney anything, and he'll do it without a second thought.

Not long ago, for example, we had a

crowd at the taping of one of our shows that exceeded the number of seats available, because we had been switched to a smaller studio at the last minute. One of my closest friends and golfing pals, Buster Hogue, was visiting me from Linton, North Dakota, at the time, and I had placed him in the front row so the folks back home could get a good look. But when so many people were denied seats, Buster promptly gave his to someone else. We managed to bring in folding chairs and get everyone seated before the show started, but Buster was still standing in the rear. So between numbers, I whispered to Barney, "Run into my dressing room and grab my chair and put it next to the brass section and we'll let Buster sit there." He did, racing offstage and returning a minute later, lugging a heavy chair. We pushed Buster into it, and if the brass section looked strange to you that night, with a handsome white-haired gentleman sitting at the end of it, now you know why! Barney was the only one in the band fast enough, willing enough—and strong enough—to race in and get that chair as he did. We all love him. I've had a tussle or two with him during the past thirty-three years, usually about his weight and his talking—Barney tries to whisper, but his whisper sounds like a strong wind blowing through the trees. I don't want to put him down, because he is one of the finest men, with one of the biggest hearts I've ever known. (I bet you thought I was going to say biggest stomach, didn't you, Barney? No, I won't say that!) I have a special, deep, lifelong affection for this slide-trombone artist, and in spite of the way I tease him occasionally, I want to say something to him right now.

Barney—don't ever change. Keep us guessing. We love you just the way you are.

Bob Lido and Joe Livoti are in our string section—Joe is our concert master, and Bob our jazz-fiddle expert and rhythm singer. Both of them are the kind of expert, dependable, solid musicians that form the strong foundation of any orchestra. I can't ever remember any kind of difference or discussion or anything but the most pleasant of relationships in over twenty years, so again, may I say—Thank you, gentlemen. It's been a great pleasure!

Now we get to the *M*'s and Richard and Mary Lou Maloof. You may know Mrs.

Maloof better as Mary Lou Metzger, my graceful and lovely dancing partner. Of course, she's a whole lot more than just my dancing partner—she's also Jack Imel's sparkling partner in their novelty song-and-dance numbers, and one of our most dependable and versatile performers. Over the years, Mary Lou has driven a train, led an elephant across the stage, sung a love song to a real live wolfhound, and made the fastest changes on record to make that last dance with me!

I love Mary Lou's relationship with her parents. They are so very proud of their "little girl," and rightfully so. It's a pleasure to see that kind of love in a family. Mary Lou and her handsome husband, Richard, are very popular with the rest of the kids. If there's a cast party or meeting or whatever, chances are it's at their house. Richard has been playing his big bass fiddle and tuba for us in superb style ever since he joined us in 1970, and both these charming young people are "wonderful, wonderful!" (There, that's one for each.)

Mickey McMahan, our strong, solid, dependable, flawless lead trumpet man, has been carrying the trumpet section since

1967. If you are getting the idea that I depend on Mickey and bless the day he joined us, you're getting the right idea. Thanks, Mickey!

The *N*'s—and Tom Netherton. Tom is well over six feet tall (six feet five, I think) and has talent to match. It seems to me his voice has only gotten better in these past eight years, and it was wonderful to start with. Tom has become one of our most popular stars, in constant demand to make personal appearances all over the country, especially at religious festivals and gatherings. It's not surprising that his beautiful rendition of sacred songs are so meaningful to his listeners. His own deep faith shines through every phrase.

Tom has built himself a beautiful home in the Glendale area, but he's seldom in town long enough to enjoy it. It doesn't matter. He loves his work so much he really enjoys traveling and meeting his fans. I might just tell you that on top of all his other attributes, he has a tremendous sense of humor. In fact, I just can't find much wrong with this thoroughly nice young man. All I can say is, Tom—it's been great to have you with us!

O is for Otwell, Roger and David. After four years, I still can't tell these fine fellows apart, but that's all right—each one is nicer than the other. Folks tell me that when they look at them, they think, "My, aren't those nice-looking boys? Don't they sing well? Don't they look as if they're honest and clean-cut and dependable, and just plain wonderful?" Well, what you see is what you get, in their case, folks. They *are* all of those nice things you see. They were a big help to Joey Schmidt when he first came on the show, and I was very grateful to them for making his path a little easier in those first few hectic months. Roger and David —whichever you are—I salute you!

Now we get to the letter *P* and Charlie Parlato, our resident Italian. Charlie is everybody's favorite. He's not very big, except for his talent and personal warmth—I sometimes think that Charlie is friendliness personified. He's another one who has been a joy to have around since the day he joined our trumpet section back in 1962.

Jack Pleis, one of our fine arrangers, is a

genius. His arrangements are truly special, always in good taste, and very easy on the ears. He's made a tremendous difference in the sound and appearance of the Aldridges and the Otwells, and he was helpful to Gail in forming her new trio, too. Jack goes with us on our tours and is of great help to all of us. I'm so glad to be in the good graces of someone who does everything just right!

And now the *R*'s. Bob Ralston is another genius, but you folks know that already. He can play, arrange, and write music for piano and organ—and as I mentioned, he dances a mean Charleston, too! Bob is also a dedicated Christian and plays many church benefits with the help of his wife, Fietje, and their two talented children, Randy and Dianne. A great talent and a truly nice man. Bob, I'm so glad I found you when you won that talent contest playing piano at age fifteen. I knew you were a winner, even then.

Curt Ramsey is another versatile talent—he sings, arranges, and is our musical librarian, too. Curt had very serious surgery for a detached retina a few years ago, but we all prayed for him, and pulled for him, and he has recovered his sight to a large degree. If Curt does something, we know it's done right. He's another whose appearance belies his age—he's been with us since the Aragon days in 1951.

And Joe Rizzo, the fourth of our arrangers, is generally regarded as the nicest "nice guy" in the band—always willing, always working, always coming through with terrific arrangements. If his eyes are red, it's not from weeping, but from putting his heart and soul into his work for us. Joe—you're wonderful!

Jim Roberts has been the ladies' favorite since our KTLA days at the Aragon in Santa Monica, way back in 1951. I think Jim has the most pleasant and easygoing personality of anyone I've ever known. If I were to tell him, "Jim—you have a big solo next week," he'd smile and say, "Fine." If I were to tell him, "Jim, we had to cancel your solo for next week," he'd smile and say, "Fine." What a disposition!

Getting close to the end of the alphabet now, with the *S*'s. Bob Smale is our resident piano-jazz genius. He can play any kind of music, and writes great arrangements, too—many of our singers ask him to do so. His technique absolutely amazes me. Bob, who has a degree from the University of California at Berkeley, is recognized as a "musician's musician." It's a great satisfaction and joy to have him with us. Bob—my heartfelt thanks.

Ah, here is Don Staples's name, and he's the kind of man I'd especially like to pay tribute to. You've heard the story of the tortoise and the hare? Well, Don is a "tortoise," and I mean that in the most complimentary of ways. Never flashy, never making a big show of himself, Don is a solidly prepared and grounded trombonist who always comes through with a top-grade performance. When I think of Don, I always think of someone smiling. That's a nice way to be remembered.

Next under the *S*'s is Kathie Sullivan, whom I found when she was still attending the University of Wisconsin. I was completely bowled over by her beautiful voice, but at first my staff didn't share my enthusiasm. Slowly, very slowly, they came over to her side, however, and the day she sang some novelty songs for us . . . Kathie was in! Now we depend on her crystalline soprano voice for everything from classics to comedy. Kathie has truly endeared herself to everyone on the show, a very lovely lady.

T is for Trimble and Turner and Thow! Kenny Trimble has played slide trombone in the orchestra for years, and I'd like to quote something he said. It made me feel good for days. Kenny and his wife were guests at our big Dedication Day in Escondido in November, and there was a great deal of television and press coverage. In a story in the San Diego *Union* newspaper the next day, Kenny was quoted as saying, "I've been with Lawrence for over thirty years, and in all that time I've never heard a harsh word from him. Not only that, he's made me a wealthy man." Kenny—may I say the same to you? And thanks, for your years of devoted service.

Jim Turner, our find from Knoxville, Tennessee, is a highly trained musician who never wanted to do anything but sing, and his big, robust voice adds greatly to our show. During the first few months he was with us, Jim came up to our home many times to work on his numbers, and it was always a joy to work with someone as gifted and eager to please as he. Jim's roots are really in Knoxville, and he flies home to see his family whenever he can; but meanwhile, his great voice is earning him many, many fans—and his dimples don't hurt, either!

George Thow is a taciturn Scotchman who is invaluable to us on our production staff. (George had to explain "taciturn" to me, but as a Harvard graduate, that was easy. He knows all about words and writes our television show for us.) He's also a former jazz trumpet man, and played in our band for several years till I put him in charge of putting words in my mouth for the show. Everybody likes this quiet gentleman who speaks only when he has something to say—and then it's either informative or funny, or both!

The *W*'s! You folks never see our announcer, Bob Warren, on the screen, but if you came to a taping of our show you'd certainly see him—tall, slender, impeccably dressed, crowned with silver-white hair and possessed of a smooth, suave manner. He warms up the audience—and by the time I walk out on stage, he's really got them primed! Most of the time when I walk out, I get a standing ovation, and I have a strong, distinct hunch that Bob is the one who has talked them into it! Bob has announced our show from the beginning, and has become more important to us with every passing year.

Rose Weiss. Ah, what can I say about this slim, trim, and lovely lady who not only designs costumes for the whole show, but makes sure I'm put together properly every week? You should see her when she comes in to inspect me in my TV outfit—putting the hankie in my pocket just so, standing back to see how I look, and making me hoist my trouser leg to make sure I've got the right color socks on! Rosie has been a dream to work with since we first went on nationwide television. She's competent, talented, and totally cooperative, and we all love her. And Rosie—I'll try to keep my socks matching.

And at last the *Z*'s! Johnny Zell embodies talent, charisma, and that certain little extra that comes from deep, committed religious faith. Along with Tom Netherton, Norma

Zimmer, Kathie Sullivan, Ava Barber, and a few other members of our group, Johnny is a dedicated Christian, and does a great deal of work for religious groups. For us, he gives his best—and those of you who have heard his trumpet know what I mean. If we had more people like Johnny, it would be easy to bring the Big Bands back. He and his beautiful young bride, Laura, often appear together on religious programs. They are a wonderful couple; and Johnny, we are so grateful to have you with us.

Norma Zimmer is the last on our list . . . and the first in our hearts. There's really nothing I could say about this lovely lady that would be equal to what all of us feel about her. She's the epitome of loveliness, kindness, goodness, and dedication. Norma's beautiful voice has endeared her not only to all of our fans since she joined us in 1960, but to many others through her work with Billy Graham. She's a grandma now, to two lovely little girls, but somehow she just keeps getting more and more beautiful as the years go by. I don't know how she does it. I only know we are all grateful for her presence in our Musical

Family. Norma, we all thank you, and kids—I love you all!

There are two gentlemen to whom I want to pay a special tribute—Sam Lutz, my manager for thirty-five years, and Don Fedderson, who has been our television consultant and syndicated-production head for all the years we have been on national television. Both of them have given me a life I could never have achieved otherwise.

Sam—or Sammy-boy, as he is sometimes known—has been with me since our days in Chicago, and he has never failed me. He's always there, always looking for the best ways to reach our goals, always helping build the band slowly and solidly, in the way I had hoped. I know that many agents and managers in this business have a reputation for not being exactly loved by their clients. But that's not the case with Sam. He was once described as a good-natured porpoise in a tank full of piranhas, and I think that's accurate. He is a truly nice man—a wonderful family man, and a doting grandpa to his two small grandchildren. Sam—I'm awfully glad you asked me to help entertain our servicemen during the war back in Chicago. It marked the beginning of a wonderful, wonderful relationship.

And Don Fedderson. Don is a television giant, who has so many hit shows to his credit I scarcely know where to begin —among them *Liberace, My Three Sons, Family Affair,* and *To Rome With Love.* Don has guided us so expertly, with such class and surety of vision over the years, I doubt if we could have made it without him. He and his public-relations expert, Les Kaufman, have also helped build the strong, secure foundation I've always wanted, and Don has been a wonderful help in forging our syndicated network. He, too, is a truly nice man. Both these gentlemen—and I use the word advisedly—are brilliant, the best in their fields, and have shared all the moments, good and bad, throughout these thirty years. Fellows, I thank you with all my heart—and I salute you!

14. My Friends Talk Back

I hope I was able to convey through those somewhat lighthearted comments in the last chapter, some of the great warmth and affection I feel for my wonderful friends, and for others whom you never see on camera—Irving Ross, our sponsor's representative and associate director on the show; tall Jim Balden, our other associate director; my old friend, Paul Weirick, who has headed our music clearance for years; Les Kaufman, our great publicity director; and Dean Kay, the superlative head of our publishing company—(and my pal when I arrive so early in the morning. Dean is usually the only one in the office at seven-thirty because he's already been talking to publishers and song-writers back east). All of them are my dear friends.

As I said in the opening of this book, it is

the "people" in your life who make the difference, and nowhere could you find proof of that more strongly than in my case! I've been lucky all my life to find people of top caliber, wonderful, devoted artists who have given unstintingly of themselves and their brilliance, adding such dimension to my life there is no way I could ever thank them.

Thinking back over our long association made me wonder what some of them thought, too, so I asked them to jot down their feelings about the pains and pleasures of working together all these years. Naturally, with the "boss" asking, I know they're going to say nothing but nice things, and I beg your indulgence in advance! But I also think you'll get some interesting and varying viewpoints and perhaps a little more understanding of the extraordinary loyalty and deep friendship among us.

Of course, we couldn't ask everyone in the band—that would have taken a whole new book! But Bernice did spend a couple of days interviewing the entire cast to get their assessments, and when we read her notes we discovered their reactions were surprisingly similar. Nearly everyone said they truly enjoyed working in a show where the emphasis was always on "pleasing the audience"—that's their first goal, too. Someone added that they felt our "product" was good. All of them said they enjoyed the feeling of family closeness, a sense that "somebody cares about us." Ken Delo put it nicely when he said ours was a "show that cares." Tom Netherton likes the fact that we provide an alternative to the regulation fare on television, something to counteract the daily dose of violence and crime. Jim Turner remarked that he enjoys the total concentration on music, pure and simple. Ron Anderson said he likes being on a show where the creative staff has "infinite knowledge of its craft," and provides a solid feeling of stability and security for the performers. And Joe Feeney said he thinks of me as his "guardian angel"! Well, thank you, Joe.

As to the "pains," almost the only comment was that it's not always possible for our singers to sing the songs they want to. But almost in the same breath, it was recognized that since the goal of the show is to play the music and sing the songs that please our wonderful audience the most, that is the criterion that decides who sings what! So it was really not a complaint as much as a recognition of what the show means. I must say I was very pleased reading these generalized comments from our Musical Family. Now I want you to read some specific comments from seven of my right-hand people. Gentlemen—and lovely lady—the pages are all yours!

Norma Zimmer

Meeting Lawrence was the happiest accident of my life! But for him, I am sure I would still be singing in a chorus somewhere, and though there is certainly nothing wrong with that, his choosing me to be on the show has not only brought me an unique happiness, it also enabled me to engage in a kind of "ministry of song" I could never have dreamed about earlier.

I had long realized that I had a non-commerical voice—an operatic-type voice not readily usable in the world of tele-vision or recordings. I wasn't unhappy about it, but I prayed often that I would use it to the best advantage. "Lord," I would pray, "You have given me this talent. Please let me find a way to use it to Your glory." Lawrence answered that prayer.

I actually met him after I was hired to sing in the chorus of a special religious recording George Cates was directing. Later, he mentioned to Lawrence that I had the kind of high soprano voice Lawrence likes, and they invited me to make a guest appearance on the show.

I was assigned just four solo lines in a religious song, but Joe Feeney, who was to sing another religious song as his solo, came down with laryngitis that day. So, instead of four bars, I wound up with a solo myself. That was a pleasant surprise, and I remember going home that night thinking what a lovely day it had been—but also thinking it was just another engagement.

But the audience response was positive, and Lawrence telephoned and invited me to sing again the next week—and the next—and the next; and then two years later, to my utter surprise, he asked me on camera, on New Year's Eve in 1960, to be the Champagne Lady. There were people watching the show that night who said my look of shock was so great it looked as if it had been rehearsed. No, that look of shock was real. I was so startled that I couldn't restrain a gasp of surprise.

211

These years with Lawrence have been the happiest of my professional life. He has been kindness itself to me, always making me feel I was special. I admire, love, and respect him completely.

Because of him I have been able to move into the field of sacred singing, which has become such a blessing in my life, and I am quite busy doing sacred concerts and church-related appearances. You might be surprised to see me in those concerts, because I am far more informal than I am on the Welk show. I walk through the audience, sing with them, trade a few jokes. My prayer is always that my singing will bring joy and will bless someone in the audience. I say the same prayer before the Welk show, also. And my daily prayer is that I myself can be a blessing to everyone I meet during that day—that I can forget myself and my problems and concentrate on the hopes and needs of others. I don't always succeed, but I do try. And I can never stop thanking God for the great gifts he has given me—my wonderful husband, Randy, our two sons, our daughter-in-law, and two lovely little granddaughters.

If it was a surprise to me to find myself on the Welk show, it is no surprise whatever to know that he is loved and adored by people as much today as he was twenty and thirty years ago. I have always felt it's because he himself loves people that his show has become so phenomenally popular. It gives him real pleasure to entertain them, and I think his genuine love for music, his joy at being with people, comes right through the television screen.

And I am not at all surprised that even in his late seventies he is still active, still busy helping his "kids" achieve their dreams. He has always seemed more concerned that the people in his "family" achieve their goals than with his own, and he loses himself trying to help them. There's a biblical injunction to the effect that "He who loses his life shall find it." I think of Lawrence that way. He has lost himself in the goodness of trying to help others, and he has found true happiness in the process.

Myron Floren

I joined Lawrence in 1950, when he was playing at the Trianon Ballroom in Chicago, and I've never been sorry, although some of my friends thought I was making a big mistake! I was performing in the St. Louis area at the time, making appearances over the local television station, and they thought I should concentrate on making a solo career of my own.

I was well aware that my little television show had opened a great many doors to me, enabling me to make appearances in areas where I wouldn't have been known otherwise. But I also knew that Lawrence and his band were broadcasting every week on a nationwide radio program, the "Miller High Life, Champagne of Bottled Beer," and I figured that playing in a band as wellknown as Lawrence's and getting that national exposure every week could only help me. So even though I took a slight cut in salary to go with him, I felt it would be the right move. As it turned out, it certainly was. (And, I might add, I have no problems with my salary now, either!)

It wasn't only my own friends who thought I was making a mistake to join Lawrence's band. There was somebody else who thought it was all wrong, too, and that was my good friend and pal, Sam Lutz. Sam was appalled, to put it mildly, when Lawrence hired me, feeling that two accordionists in one band was one accordionist too many.

But I doubt if Lawrence gave a thought to the fact that he would have a little competition within his own band. What interested him then—and interests him now—is presenting the best possible show. That has always been his paramount interest, and I've always admired the fact that he is totally dedicated to his main goal in life, which is to do the best show possible for the audience who will be watching it.

Actually, I would say that he and I share some of the same qualities—for good or bad! He's a stubborn German and I'm an equally stubborn Norwegian. We both share a total commitment to whatever we're doing, and both want to do our best at all times.

I think of Lawrence more as an administrator, a director, a supersalesman, who is more interested in developing a depth of talent within the band than in promoting himself. I believe that one of the reasons the other big bands failed when they were exposed to the weekly scrutiny of a television show is because there were only one or perhaps two stars in the show. Lawrence has developed a whole company of "stars," and this deep support, this "family" concept, has given the show a depth and richness it could never have achieved otherwise. He has stuck to his primary goal of entertaining people, but the odd thing is that by developing the talents of others and pushing them into the limelight, he has emerged as the biggest star of all! There's a lesson there somewhere.

I like the fact that he's always optimistic. I'm the same way myself. I'm always sure that whatever happens is for the best. If one door closes, two more will open. I'm still that way, and right now I have more projects on the fire than ever before.

You may have heard I suffered from rheumatic fever as a child, and was off the show for three weeks in 1975 with a case of subacute bacterial endocarditis. But with the fine doctors and medical treatment available today, I not only recovered, but the doctors tell me my heart is in the best condition it has ever been. I jog, and do aerobic exercises, but I would say my work alone keeps me physically fit. I fly out of town on personal appearances almost every week after the show is over, and when you're squeezing that accordion hours and hours every day as I do, it keeps you in pretty good shape!

I play perhaps two hundred dates a year, including about sixty dance dates in places like the Willowbrook Ballroom in Chicago, and I've noticed that the crowds are increasing. There seems to be a renewed interest in the beautiful ballroom dances of the forties, and it is even being said that the Big Bands are coming back. If so, we'll be ready! As Lawrence says, "We've been here all along. We never left."

Lawrence has asked a few of us who have been with him for many years to talk about the pains and pleasures of working with him on the show. I can honestly say the pleasures have been many, and the pains —none at all. These years have been wonderful for me, the most productive, exciting, and rewarding of my life. My wife, Berdyne, and I have raised five lovely daughters. Our daughter Kristie, as you perhaps know, is married to Bobby Burgess, and we now have a beautiful little granddaughter, Becki, and a handsome grandson, Robert Floren Burgess. God has blessed me abundantly, and I am deeply grateful for the blessings He has showered on me and my family.

I'm known as an easy crier in the band,

and it's true I'm emotional and I shed a few tears when I am moved. But I can shed no tears thinking of these wonderful Welk years. I'm just grateful with all my heart that Lawrence decided he wanted another accordionist in the band. (And it's nice to know that Sam now agrees with him!)

Jim Hobson

". . . And I Learned About Show Business From This . . ."

Don Fedderson, the man responsible for putting Lawrence Welk on network television, and Sam Lutz, Lawrence's personal manager for thirty-four years, and I were having dinner one evening when the discussion of how to better publicize the Lawrence Welk Show came up. After kicking around several ideas Don said, "I don't know, Jim. How do you publicize a household word?" And that's the spot I'm in. I have been asked to say a few words about my twenty-six years working as director and, since 1962, producer-director of the Welk show. How do you condense a professional career-span of 26 years working with a living legend into a few

218

words? I guess the only way is to start at the beginning, and the beginning is the man and his philosophy toward show business —in this case, his television show.

I first met Lawrence in Sam Lutz's office in the summer of 1955. Of course, I'd known of Lawrence for years. I had been working for Don Fedderson, then general manager of KLAC-TV, Channel 13, in Los Angeles since January of 1949, and had worked up through the ranks to producing and directing his two most popular shows: "The Liberace Show" and Cliff Stone's "Hometown Jamboree," starring Tennessee Ernie. My agent, Harold Jovien, asked me if I would like to direct the Lawrence Welk Show on the ABC network, starting in July, and of course I jumped at the opportunity. Here was the chance of a lifetime—a local television director being entrusted to direct a very successful local television show on a national network, a chance all local directors dream of but few get. In the office that day were Ed Sobol, the producer, recently program manager of NBC; and a man of vast experience in legitimate theater, motion pictures, and television: Sam Lutz; and of course, Lawrence. Introductions were made and I nervously sat down, wondering how best to impress this awe-inspiring trio of show-business experts. A heavy silence settled over the room. Finally Ed Sobol said, "This director doesn't talk much, does he?" I retreated further into my self-consciousness, knowing I'd lost the chance of a lifetime. Lawrence looked me right in the eyes and said quietly, "Jim, how would you shoot a banjo player?" Startled back to reality, I rattled off something like . . . "Oh, I'd put him on a stool in a spotlight, start with a head-to-toe shot so you could identify him, and then do a series of closeups of his face, hands, etc., to show the audience all the intricacies of his musical ability." That did it. Lawrence is a great believer in closeups . . . "Show me the wrinkles on the faces. I want to see their eyes, their expressions, and their technique." His obsession with closeups led to an amusing incident a few months after we started the show. It was Tuesday morning and I was in the studio staging the opening number. A few minutes before camera rehearsal was to start, Lawrence came bounding up to me full of enthusiasm and said, "Chim" . . . (he had a slight accent) . . . "I had the greatest idea driving into the studio just now. I want you to get me a closeup of the *whole band!*"

Lawrence has four rules we all live by. "Play the melody" . . . (George Cates, our musical director's, responsibility). "Take lots of closeups" . . . (mine). "Be on time" . . . (everybody's. He's a real stickler for that). And "Keep it simple." The last two have been my hardest-fought personal battles.

Being on time is not one of my strong points. I have a pretty good imagination and a bad tendency to try and cram too many things into too short a time span. "Keeping it simple" is another. I love production numbers and often get carried away trying to do too much. In fact Lawrence once said to me, "You know Jim, you have a tendency to start with the complicated and work toward the simple solution. Why don't you try it the other way 'round—and start with the simple?"

Well, there you have it. I've worked with Lawrence for twenty-six wonderful years, learning, growing, trying to keep it simple—and be on time! Thanks, Lawrence. It couldn't have come from a nicer guy.

Sam Lutz

In 1944, I was in charge of Special Services, arranging entertainment for the wounded soldiers in Gardner General Hospital in Chicago. It was a vital job in the sense that many of the boys were in very low spirits, some so depressed they didn't want to live. I rounded up some of the top names in the business to entertain them, and one day I called on Lawrence, who was then playing at the Trianon and Aragon Ballrooms in Chicago. He agreed to come over to the hospital and brought his Champagne Lady, Jayne Walton, and the entire band. I couldn't help but notice how strongly the young soldiers in the audience responded to him and his music. They had enjoyed the other entertainers, of course—the Andrews Sisters, Sophie Tucker, Tommy Dorsey, other big bands of the day. But Lawrence's warmth and charisma seemed to be exactly what they needed, and I called on him again and again after that. He never refused.

After the war I went to Los Angeles. Like thousands of other G.I.'s, I was looking for a job. I had been Henry Busse's personal manager for ten years prior to the war—and we often played the Chez Paree in Chicago,

222

the number one nightclub in the world. Now, in Los Angeles, I ran into a friend who told me Lawrence was playing at the Aragon Ballroom on Lick Pier in Santa Monica and had mentioned that he thought he remembered me from Chicago and could possibly use me as his personal manager. I went down that same evening and stood at the edge of the bandstand, smiling hopefully till Lawrence recognized me—I looked a little different out of uniform. We chatted and Lawrence suggested we meet for breakfast the next morning for further discussion. "Fine," I said. "What time?" "Six o'clock," he said matter-of-factly. My jaw dropped. For someone like me, used to the late hours of orchestras and nightclubs, six o'clock in the morning seemed like the middle of the night. But I was there! In fact, I was fifteen minutes early. We talked, and Lawrence finally asked me how much I wanted. "Well," I said, "a one-hundred-dollar draw against commissions." He turned pale. There was no way he could pay me one hundred dollars, as I soon found out. He was barely clearing that much himself, after paying the band salaries and expenses. We talked it over and finally agreed on a twenty-five-dollar weekly draw.

I was glad to get it! I really needed a job.

For the next few years, I arranged bookings out of our Los Angeles office while Lawrence and the band traveled on the road. But in 1951, he came to Los Angeles and made his television debut over KTLA. I had been trying for weeks to reach Klaus Landsberg, manager of KTLA, to see if he would put the band on the air. I could never get through to him on the phone, but one night, quite by accident, I reached him at his home. Talking fast, I explained what I wanted and he finally agreed to put the band on the air if Lawrence would pay the band expenses.

On the night of the broadcast, I sat out in the camera car with Mr. Landsberg, who was widely regarded as a genius in the field, watching Lawrence and the band on the tiny TV monitor in the truck. I thought the show went very well, and afterward I said, "Mr. Landsberg—would you put the band on the air next week, too?" "Aaaaah," he said, gruffly, reaching for the phone and dialing KTLA, "I'll have to think about that." The line to KTLA was busy and it stayed busy for the next half hour—Mr. Landsberg must have called twenty times. When he finally got through, the switchboard girl cried, "We're going crazy here, Mr. Landsberg, we're swamped with calls about that Welk band, people want to know if it's going to be on the air every week. Is it?" Landsberg looked over at me, grinned a little, and said, "Yeah . . . I think maybe it is."

We stayed on the air for the next four weeks, left Los Angeles to fulfill a previous booking in St. Louis, and returned to KTLA, where we continued to broadcast from the Aragon every week for the next four years. Then, as Lawrence has told you, we went on national television over ABC on July 2, 1955, marking the debut of the longest-running musical show in television history.

I'm proud to be associated with Lawrence. I knew, when I first saw him in Chicago, that he had something special, a charisma, a human quality that people responded to. He is completely honest in all his dealings, and has built a career on trust. When we made our first deal over the breakfast table back in 1945, we drew up a rough agreement for one year. At the end of that time, Lawrence said, "Sam, we don't need this. Let's just shake hands." That handshake sealed a bargain on a partnership that is still flourishing, thirty-five years later.

Don Fedderson

When I first told Lawrence that the Dodge Motor Company had agreed to sponsor him on a thirteen-week summer replacement show on the ABC network, his eyes filled with tears. "Oh, Don," he said huskily, "that's wonderful—wonderful! Now, we'll have to find a good-looking young announcer to lead the band, someone who can talk really well."

I just looked at him. Finally I said, "Lawrence—they don't want anybody else to lead the band. They want you!"

He looked panic-stricken as I tried to convince him that all the things he thought were drawbacks—his accent, his shyness, his sometimes quaint way of expressing himself—were actually assets. "People can relate to you, they feel comfortable with you," I told him. I don't know that I convinced him, but I do know that when the show went on the air, his natural warmth and sincerity came through the national television screens just as powerfully

226

as they had on his local show in Los Angeles. By the end of that thirteen-week series, we had jumped from a rating of 7.2 to the high 20s, and were firmly embarked on a weekly series which is now going into its twenty-seventh consecutive year. They have been twenty-seven wonderful years.

When I first saw Lawrence on television on KTLA, in the early fifties, I was president of San Francisco's KYA, and KLAC in Los Angeles, but I was so impressed with his potential, I was certain he would enjoy a fine television future. Los Angeles is a microcosm of the entire country, populated by people from every state in the Union and I felt that his great popularity in the Los Angeles area was a good indication he would be equally popular in the country as a whole.

I contacted his personal manager, Sam Lutz, and we met with Lawrence to discuss the idea. It was decided to produce a pilot film to show to prospective sponsors, and Les Kaufman, then with Grant Advertising, worked with me producing a presentation book bearing the legend "The Man With the Golden Touch," detailing Lawrence's many achievements in the world of music. Sam and I took the book and film to

227

Chicago to show to the Grant Advertising Agency. Will Grant liked what he saw and we flew to Detroit and sold the Lawrence Welk Show to Bill Newburg, president of the Dodge Division of the Chrysler Corporation as a summer replacement to begin July 2, 1955.

Lawrence understandably was terrified during those first few broadcasts: the shows were live, with no chance to correct mistakes; and for many seasons, he and I would sit together in the back row of the empty studio going over his lines while the band rehearsed on stage. His ear was always on the music, however, and he would frequently dash on stage to correct a tempo or change a musical phrase. His feel for his music has always been flawless, as is his ability to pace a show. I remember how astonished I was the first time I saw him schedule a jazz number, follow it with a hymn, and then a contemporary ballad. But his instincts in such matters are infallible and he is keenly attuned to what his audience enjoys most.

In my long career, I have been privileged and fortunate to produce "The Millionaire," "The Liberace Show," "My Three Sons," "Family Affair," "Do You Trust

Your Wife?" "Date with the Angels," "The Smith Family," "To Rome With Love," and "Who Do You Trust?" among other shows, and I've enjoyed working with some of show business's finest stars: Henry Fonda, Johnny Carson, Liberace, Brian Keith, John Forsythe, Sebastian Cabot, Edgar Bergen, Walter Brennan, Bill Frawley, Bill Demarest, Betty White, and many others. And perhaps the most satisfying aspect of my work has been to find exactly the right person for the right role. I was fortunate, for example, to find Fred MacMurray to play the father in "My Three Sons," William Frawley as "Bub," the boys' grandfather, and later, William Demarest as Uncle Charley. And I remember thinking, when I first saw Lawrence on television, that his warmth and sincerity would make him an ideal "man-next-door," someone whose qualities of compassion and decency and good humor and honesty would exemplify all that's best in our American character. Time, and our close personal relationship, have proven my instincts were right. However, in Lawrence's case, art imitates life. He really *is* all the qualities we so admire.

Lawrence was cast by life for his role.

Lon Varnell

I had the privilege of seeing Mr. Welk perform in person for the first time when my wife and I went to his concert in Chattanooga, Tennessee, in 1962. I've been a promoter for many years and accustomed to dealing with great stars, but never had I seen anyone hold an audience like Mr. Welk, or bring greater joy and happiness to them. He seemed to embody all the qualities I admire most, and I knew I wanted to present him and his wonderful Musical Family at the very first opportunity.

But that wasn't quite as easy as it sounds. A great many other people wanted to present him, too, as I found out when I contacted his manager, Mr. Sam Lutz, and it took two years of telephone calls and letters before Mr. Sam finally allowed me to book Mr. Welk for one concert. (I found out later that this is typical of Mr. Welk. He never enters anything without thoroughly investigating it and making sure it's a worthwhile venture from every side, insofar as it's possible to predict.)

I was very, very nervous about that first

concert, which was in my hometown of Nashville, Tennessee. I wanted everything to be just perfect for Mr. Welk, and I was elated that it turned out well enough that Mr. Sam weakened and gave me three concert dates the following year.

I was delighted, and it was during that short tour that I had the opportunity to get to know Mr. Welk a little better. On the morning of our second day, I got up early, as is my habit, and went out for a walk, and there was Mr. Welk, sitting on a park bench enjoying the early morning sunshine. He invited me to sit down and we got to talking, and after a while he said, "You know, it's foolish for you to rent a room for yourself, and another big, expensive suite just for me. Why don't you take the extra bedroom in my suite?"

"Oh, Mr. Welk," I said, "I couldn't do that."

"Why not?" he asked, reasonably.

"Well," I said, floundering a little, "I . . . I don't want to intrude."

"You wouldn't be intruding," he said briskly. "It would save you a little money and it would be more convenient for both of us."

Finally I agreed, and to this day we are

still "roommates" on tour.

That particular tour went well enough that Sam gave me five dates the following year, and at the end of the tour, Mr. Welk said, "Lon—I've been discussing this with Sam and we want you to handle all our tour dates. You be the boss from now on."

(Lawrence talking: I'm going to interrupt Lon at this point to say that I asked him to take over the tours because never in my many years in show business had I come across a man who did things as well, as efficiently, as honestly, or as perfectly as Lon did! Tours can sometimes be upsetting, but with Lon at the helm, we had nothing to worry about and I made up my mind not to lose him. Now, back to you, Lon!)

After that, we began taking Mr. Welk and his fine orchestra on tours two or three times a year although for the last few years we have limited ourselves to just two—a ten-day tour in March throughout the South, and another in June throughout the North. It's interesting to note that most performers have certain areas in the nation where they are very strong, and they tend to avoid the sections where they are weak. But with the Russ Morgan band. But it wasn't till he came to Los Angeles and began televising over KTLA from the Aragon Ballroom in Santa Monica that we picked up our friendship and began working together.

After I had directed a few recording sessions for him, Lawrence asked me if I would be interested in becoming his musical director and rehearsing the band. "I need somebody like you," he said. "You have the musical knowledge and know-how that could be of real help to us, and I think you can make a big improvement in the band." The idea appealed to me and, since I could schedule my own recording sessions at Coral, I knew I could arrange to give him one day a week. "How much would you want?" he asked. "Well," I said, "I would ordinarily handle several recording sessions during the day—why don't you just pay me what I would have made here at the studio?"

That sounded reasonable to him. "And how much would that be?" he wanted to know. "One hundred dollars a day," I told him.

There was a pause—a long one. Then he said, "Let me think that over,

Mr. Welk has strong fan support in all parts of the country, no matter where we go. In Florida, it is even stronger. Generally speaking, we play one concert per year in one major city in each state, but we are always obliged to play more in Florida, and in 1981 we played eight concerts in four days, something almost unheard of in our profession.

The only other artist I have ever known who elicited the same devoted response from his fans as Mr. Welk was Elvis Presley. Both these artists enjoyed a tremendous rapport with their audiences, and Mr. Welk today has the strongest ties with his audience of anyone I have ever known.

There are many reasons for this. First of all, he truly enjoys direct contact with his fans. Many performers do not enjoy it— they shy away from it, feeling the lack of privacy is a terrible price to pay. They don't want to spend time giving autographs or chatting with their fans. But Mr. Welk has a great impulse to give—and receive —love. That includes people of all ages. His greatest fans are the older people, that is true, and I believe he brings them a warmth and love they need very badly. I cannot think of any other contemporary artist who takes the time to cater to their needs, bring them the music they enjoy, and make them feel that somebody really cares about them like he does.

But younger people respond to him, too. When we were in Birmingham, Alabama, recently, the Welk people were staying at the same hotel as a sorority convention of teenage girls, and when Mr. Welk and I attempted to walk into the lobby one afternoon, the rush for autographs was so great we had to move out onto the street. Mr. Welk stood and signed autographs—I estimated about twelve hundred—for approximately two hours. He never complained at standing there so long. Rather, he seemed to be thanking the people who asked, showing sincere interest in each of them. Mr. Welk is secure within himself, and this radiates strength and security to others. I have seen him take a frightened singer by the hand, onstage in front of fifteen thousand people, and somehow transfer his own calm confidence to them so they lose their stage fright completely. I think this kind of security is very attractive to people, and is another reason they flock to him. And I would say

his inner security comes from his roots. must have had a very fine and lo upbringing. His qualities of integ compassion, and complete dedicatio whatever he does are a testament to th cherish our friendship, which began so ago on that park bench in the early m sunshine. Over the years we have disc we are in complete accord on all ou philosophical and ethical beliefs, believe with all my heart that th Lord brought us together. We both in the same kind of wholesom tainment and, in my opinion, contributed as much to our societ way of bringing joy and happi people who sorely need it, as any world.

George Cates

I first worked with Lawrence a in 1951, when they were record Records, and I was the A (Artists and Records) for the had known Lawrence earlie met when he was playing Penn Hotel in Pittsburgh,

will you, George?''

Next day he telephoned and said one hundred dollars would be fine and I went to work as his musical director. That was thirty years ago, and just recently he said to me, ''George, I've done a lot of things in my life that were lucky, but I think the luckiest was when I hired you. And you know—I almost backed out when you said one hundred dollars! You have to understand, George, that it wasn't so long before that that the whole band and I together were earning one hundred dollars a day!!''

It's been a wonderful relationship. Lawrence has been with me through some of the happiest times of my life, as well as the most traumatic. We had been working on the network TV show for only thirteen weeks when I was stricken with a massive heart attack, and spent the next two weeks under an oxygen tent. It was another few months before I got back full time with the show, but Lawrence never wavered in his faith that I would recover. You might be interested to know that my heart attack was the origin of my beard. When I was critically ill, I was not allowed to be shaven, of course, and later the ban was still on because I was being injected with blood-

237

thinning drugs and the slightest nick or cut could have caused a hemorrhage. I was planning to shave my beard off, but one day my doctor told me I would have to make a conscious effort to move and walk more slowly until I was fully recovered. ''When you find you are walking too fast, just touch your beard,'' he suggested. ''That will remind you to move more slowly.'' I did as he said, and by the time I had gotten back to normal, I decided to keep my beard as a good-luck omen.

I'm grateful for that heart attack in some ways. It demonstrated very dramatically to me what the real priorities of life are. My family had always been vitally important to me, but after that they meant even more, and I began to use my time to better advantage. I've always like to read, and I love to go to symphony concerts or attend new plays and musicals. I think those things add to my understanding as a musician, and I resolved to do more of that. I also came out of that heart attack with a different attitude toward life. I am content now with my own values, my own role in life.

I'm not the kind of person who wants or needs everybody to like me. I want them to respect me, true, and where the band and I are concerned, I think we have a mutual respect. Some of the finest, most accomplished musicians in the business are in our band today, and it is a genuine pleasure to work with them.

I want to tell you one incident about Lawrence which I think demonstrates not only the depth of our friendship, but his sensitive response to other people's feelings. When my first wife, Ruth, died in 1973, I was in a terrible state of depression for many months. I couldn't seem to snap out of my grief, no matter how I tried. One day Lawrence called, expressing sympathy, and said, "George—I'm getting a little older and I need more help with the band. I thought perhaps if you were to help me conduct—take over some of my chores—it would not only help me . . . it might give you a new interest in life. What do you say?" That started my coming from behind the camera to conducting in front, and he couldn't have done anything that helped me more. Conducting the band—which I've always loved to do, being on stage, trying to entertain people—began to lift my veil of depression, and I was finally able to accept Ruth's death and go on living with renewed interest. Because of that, I was able to meet my beautiful Miriam, and when that happened, my "cure" was complete. It is something of a miracle to me that Miriam came into my life. She knew and loved Ruth, too. Her children and mine are compatible. We have forged a new family together, and these last few years have been full of happiness for both of us. Lawrence and Fern attended our wedding, and have become dear friends. We go to Escondido together, have dinner together, and—in the years we were playing Tahoe—Fern and Miriam played the slot machines together!

Let me tell you the other incident about Lawrence that demonstrates the kind of man he is.

I belong to the Eddie Cantor Chapter of the B'nai B'rith Lodge in Los Angeles, and one of our main interests is supporting the Israel Levin Center for Senior Citizens in Venice, California, a nearby beach town. We provide food at minimal prices so the seniors are able to get at least one hot meal a day, and we often visit them. Last year Irving Ross, who is associate director of our show and an ex-president of the Lodge, and his wife, Lenore, and Miriam and I went to visit the Center one Sunday. When we walked in, the folks recognized me from the show and pushed me up on stage to say a few words. Before I could begin, however, someone shouted from the rear of the room, "What are you doing here?"

Startled, I said, "What am I doing here? I'm a member of the Eddie Cantor Lodge —that's what I'm doing here!"

"You can't be a member of the Lodge!" the man shot back. "You work for Lawrence Welk—and everybody knows Welk doesn't hire Jews!"

I was shocked, but then I said, as evenly as I could, "That's a ridiculous statement. It has absolutely no basis in fact—and I'd like to set the record straight right now." And for the next few minutes I did.

"First of all," I said, "I *am* a Jew. Secondly, I have known and worked closely with Lawrence Welk for thirty years . . . and in all that time I have never known him to display any semblance of anti-Semitism whatsoever, either covertly or overtly.

"You say he won't hire Jews. Well . . . thirty years ago he hired me. And almost thirty-five years ago he hired Sam J. Lutz as his personal manager—and I think you'll agree that Sam Lutz sounds like he might be Jewish! Lawrence's first producer in television was a Jew—Ed Sobol, who has since passed away. Harry Hyams, who plays viola in the band, is Jewish. So is Russ Klein, featured saxophonist in the band, who is married to Lawrence's secretary of thirty-four years, Lois Lamont."

By this time the room was absolutely quiet. "Standing right over there," I said, "is Irving Ross—you all know him. He's been the sponsor representative on the Welk show since 1960, and associate director since 1979. And then there's Rose Weiss, our costume designer. Rosie not only does costumes for the entire band and the singers, she has also selected Lawrence's wardrobe for the past twenty-two years, and believe me, he wears what she tells him!

"And one thing more," I said, quietly, "Lawrence's principal sponsor for twenty years, until his death last August, was Matty Rosenhaus, chairman of the board of the J. B. Williams Company. Mr. Rosenhaus was not only one of the greatest Jewish philanthropists of our time, he was also a prime mover in the B'nai B'rith Anti-Defamation League. Now do you think a man like Mr. Rosenhaus, a devout and caring Jew, would have anything to do with Lawrence if he were anti-Semitic?"

I added—and I really felt every word,

"The only basis on which Lawrence Welk hires people is their ability. Their religion or race has nothing to do with it and never has. I hate to hear this rumor because it hurts a fine man and an entire organization, for no reason at all."

When I finished, many of the people in the room were in tears, and at first I thought maybe I had spoken too harshly. But they were crying for joy. They swarmed around me, telling me they had always loved the show but felt guilty about watching it because of the stories they had heard about Lawrence. "Now," said one little old lady, grabbing my hand and covering it with kisses, "now I can watch and enjoy!"

I was upset by the incident and I told Lawrence about it. He was troubled, too. "Would you like to go and visit those folks, Lawrence?" I asked him. "I think it would mean a lot to them." "Yes, I would," he said, "whenever you can arrange it."

Next Sunday we all returned to the Center, and again, as I walked in, the folks greeted me. This time when I went up on stage I said, "Some of you told me last time I was here you'd like to have Lawrence

Welk visit you in person. Did you really mean that?"

The whole room began clapping, so I said, "Would you like him to come soon?" "Yes," they shouted in union. "How about right now?" I asked. And that was Lawrence's cue to walk through the door, playing his accordion. For the next hour he brought those folks some of the happiest moments of their lives. It was a pleasure to watch. He played their favorite songs, danced with the ladies, talked to them, hugged them, and when he left, it was as a loved "member of the family."

To me this is a very important story, not only because it demonstrates the warmth and beauty of Lawrence's nature, but because it lays to rest a vicious and untrue rumor. When we tried to figure out how it got started, the only thing we could think of was that the Lennon sisters, who starred on the show for twelve years, are devout Catholics, as is Lawrence, and maybe people assumed you had to be Catholic to be on the show. From there, it was only a short step to assume you couldn't be Jewish. But, of course, both assumptions are one hundred percent wrong.

Bigotry and anti-Semitism are wrong and

evil. But it's also evil to falsely accuse someone, and I wanted to share this true story with you.

And one other thing. I know Lawrence has written in some of his other books that I've been known to raise my voice on occasion. I accept that. And I'd like to raise it again right now and say, "Lawrence —Shalom . . . and Mazel Tov! Peace—and my heartfelt thanks."

15. The Champagne Ladies

When I was talking about my friends a chapter or so ago, I left out a very important group—and you'll see why in a moment. I'm talking about the Champagne Ladies, who have dressed up our orchestra and warmed our hearts for almost fifty years.

The first Champagne Lady, although she didn't wear that title, was Maxine Gray, a charming, sparkling, friendly girl who was a great asset to us in the early days as we traveled on the road. Her mother traveled with us and I used to love to tease her by hinting that Maxine had fallen in love with someone she had met at one of the dances and was planning to leave the business. "Maxine!" her mother would cry. "You forget that nonsense and keep on singing!" Years later, when I fell ill in California,

Maxine and her husband took me into their home and nursed me back to health. Maxine is still a good friend and we often talk to her (and to her mother, who has long since forgiven me my teasing—I hope!).

Next was Lois Best, the first girl singer to wear the Champagne Lady title. That was in Pittsburgh at the William Penn Hotel, where we first came up with the name Champagne Music. Lois was a beautiful young girl who fell in love with our trumpeter, Jules Herman. I guess I've always been something of a tease, because I waited till Lois was within earshot and then told somebody a long story about how Jules was already married and had several children. Of course he wasn't, but poor Lois was devastated till she found out I had made the whole thing up. She and Jules were married and now live in St. Paul, where Jules has a band of his own. They are wonderful people and we are often in touch.

Jayne Walton took over then, and of all the Champagne Ladies, she was the closest to my family. Jaynie had a wonderful Irish sense of humor, and used to kid me unmercifully about being from the farm.

She still has an Irish sense of humor—and still kids me! Our families have stayed quite close over the years. Jayne writes to Fern and me regularly, and I see her whenever the show plays near San Antonio, Texas, where she now lives.

After Jayne came pert and pretty Roberta Linn. She was a big favorite with the crowds who came to the Aragon Ballroom on Lick Pier in Santa Monica, and had much to do with our television popularity in those early years—I can still hear her little trademark giggle. Roberta is still active in the business, singing at supper clubs and fair dates.

After Roberta Linn came the late and lovely Alice Lon. Yes, we lost little Alice last spring, when she passed on at her home in Texas. We were all saddened by her passing, but she left many beautiful memories. Alice was the first Champagne Lady on national television and became famous for her big, frilly skirts with ruffled petticoats. She was a wonderful little dancer as well as a good singer. It's odd how many of our very best girl singers came from Texas. Maxine, Jayne, Alice, and our Ralna of today are all from Texas and all have remarkable voices. I was playing some old records of Jayne and Alice just the other day, and we remarked on what wonderful band singers they were. I've been lucky all my life in finding Champagne Ladies who were not only ladies and attractive and wholesome, but fine singers, too.

After Alice came our lovely Norma Zimmer, and I've already mentioned how we feel about her. She's just perfection.

All the Champagne Ladies added a great deal to my life—and the life of our Musical Family—but, as you may have noticed, not one of them has been willing to stay with me permanently, week in and week out. Only one. My own personal Champagne Lady, the lovely girl I married fifty years ago, the mother of my children, and the Queen of our home. My wife, Fern.

16. Fern

When Fern and I celebrated our Golden Wedding Anniversary on April 18th of this year, I couldn't believe it. How could fifty years have vanished so swiftly? Where had they gone? It seemed like only yesterday that we had stood together in the dim quietness of Sacred Heart Cathedral in Sioux City, Iowa, and recited our vows in the first flush of the morning's light. It was only five o'clock in the morning when a young priest named Father Leo McCoy united us in marriage—and if you wonder why we chose that unearthly hour to be wed, well, that's the practical side of the Welks coming through! Fern's train arrived from Dallas, Texas, at four in the morning, and we had to be on the road by ten that same morning in order to make our next booking that night, so five o'clock was the only time we could schedule a wedding mass.

Our wedding was very small—only Fern and I; our attendants, Dr. and Mrs. Frank Abst; and the priest. My little band had tried valiantly to attend, but they had all fallen asleep in the car outside waiting for the church to open and the service to begin! Afterward, however, we all got together and went to the Martin Hotel for a small wedding breakfast, and then Fern and I set out on the first lap of a journey that has taken us fifty years so far. And, just as our wedding was small and intimate, so was our Golden Wedding celebration. Just our family. Nothing could have been more perfect.

When I first realized this momentous occasion was approaching, I began thinking about a mammoth party to celebrate the event, but my bride shook her head. "No," she said, in tones I recognized from long experience meant Don't argue! "I don't want a big party. I just want our own family to be together for this occasion."

All our children honored her wishes and for weeks and months before the big day, Shirley and Larry and Donna spent hours on the phone, writing letters, making plans, and completing the arrangements. All our children and grandchildren came home for the party. Donna and her husband, Jim, and their youngest children, Christine and David, flew in from Boise a few days beforehand. Their eldest son, Jimmy, who is at Stanford, along with Shirley and Bob's son, David, flew in too, as did our eldest grandchild, Laura, who came all the way from the University of Illinois. Shirley's other two sons, Robbie and Jonathan, drove up from Occidental College and the University of San Diego, respectively, but Larry's boys, Lawrence Welk the Third and Kevin, didn't have quite so far to go—just over the hill from the San Fernando Valley.

The day of the celebration dawned wild, wet, and windy, a very untypical California April day. I lounged in bed in the morning —something very untypical of me—listening to the rain beat against the panes outside, and reflecting on the unbelievable fact that Fern and I had shared fifty years together. It still seems something of a miracle to me that she ever agreed to marry me in the first place. It took me two years of intensive persuasion to convince her to say yes. You really couldn't blame her. She was a nurse in training, and wanted to be a doctor, something almost unheard of for a young lady in those years. She wasn't the least bit interested in the music business and she was afraid—and justly so—that my profession might not be too stable. She wanted substance in her life, not just good times. I think she was surprised, when she got to know me a little better, to find out that was what I wanted, too. I enjoyed a good time, true, and music is so much a part of my life I couldn't live without it. But I, too, wanted a life of substance, and a wife who was dependable, loyal, and willing to work for our mutual goals, someone whose basic religious and philosophical ethics were the same as mine. Fern was all of these—and besides, she was very, very pretty!

I wasn't too sure just what kind of a party the children were planning for us beyond the fact that it would be at Shirley's home and start at four o'clock in the afternoon. "What shall I wear?" I asked Fern, along about three. "Oh, just one of your nice dark suits," she said. I got dressed as instructed and sat waiting for her in our living room, which was beginning to resemble a florist's shop from the many beautiful flowers and plants our friends had sent us. I was riffling through a stack of congratulatory cards and wires when Fern walked in, dressed in a long, flowing formal gown of pale chiffon and looking lovely as a bride. "Wow!" I said, appreciatively. "Beautiful! Is that a white gown?" "No," she said, eyes sparkling, "it's champagne chiffon!" I thought that was very nice of her and told her so as I handed her carefully into our car for the short drive to Shirley's home.

When we arrived, all the children were there, gathered together in the living room, dressed in their best, and smiling warmly in welcome, along with Father John Carroll, a priest from St. Paul the Apostle Church and a friend of Shirley and her family. I looked around that room—at our three children, their spouses, our ten lovely grandchildren—and I was overwhelmed. I have been surrounded by love all my life—not only by my mother and father and brothers and sisters and by Fern and our own family, but by hundreds of thousands of wonderful, unnamed and loving people all across this land. Our loyal fans have brought us an affection and regard that have meant the world to me, and I value it highly. But nothing can match the love of your own family, and standing there in our daughter's living room with our children all around us, I felt surrounded, washed, bathed in love.

But if they had asked me to express my feelings, I could never have done it—you know by now what a hard time I have doing that! Fortunately for me, Father Carroll took over and officiated at a brief ceremony that was so lovely I want to repeat part of it for you. First, he stood and lighted candles and then invoked God's blessing on our Golden Wedding Anniversary. Then Larry stood to recite a passage from the book of Genesis which spoke of the creation of man; Donna followed with a psalm of Thanksgiving; Jonathan read the letter of Paul to the Corinthians, those noble and blessed words which describe the power of love so beautifully; and Father Carroll spoke of the miracle our Lord performed at the wedding feast in Cana, and of the tremendous importance of families in our life. He said: "If we lost all our copies of the Bible, and all our written records, we would still have the ancient faith—so long as we had families."

Shirley read the Prayer of St. Francis —long one of my favorites—and then began a part of the day that will stay forever in my heart. Each one of our children and grandchildren spoke, right from where they were sitting, each one in turn, spontaneously in most cases, although some of the younger children had written out their thoughts. They told of their warm feelings for Fern and me, and their prayers and hopes for us. If we weren't all weeping before that part of the celebration was over, I would be very surprised! I know I was, as I listened to each of our dear ones say such loving and kind things about us. Larry ended by saying, "I want you both to know that my love for you grows every day." By that time I really was dissolved in tears, but "Buns"—that's Lawrence Welk the Third —came to my rescue by announcing matter-of-factly that "Grandma is the perfect Grandma and I love to come to her house because she's such a good cook!" And little brother Kevin seconded the motion by adding, "And she makes the *best* mashed potatoes!"

Then Father Carroll said, "Mr. and Mrs. Welk—are you ready to renew the commitment you have already been living for fifty years?" He asked us to stand and hold hands and recite the vows we had taken so many years earlier. He asked: "Have you both come here freely and of your own accord to pledge your love to each other—and renew your vows?" I said, "We have." Then he said: "And with God's help will you continue loving each other, and your children, and your grandchildren, in all the days that God gives you?" There was a slight pause, and then I said loudly, "Well, *I* will!"

All the love and tension and tears that had been building in the past half hour spilled over into a wave of laughter, and Father said, twinkling, "Well, how about you, Mrs. Welk? Will you do that, too?" "Yes," said Fern, laughing, "I will!" "There," said the priest, "it's in the record." "And I pressed it out of her," I added.

We began to repeat the vows, as Father recited them—"To have and to hold . . . for better or worse . . . for richer or poorer . . ." Those words had meant a great deal to me when I first heard them. Listening to them now, after a lifetime of struggle and hardship, of great happiness and unexpected joys, a lifetime in which love had solved all our problems, I realized anew how beautiful and transcendent those vows are. We concluded the service with a litany of praise and then sang "We Gather Together," as Shirley accompanied us at the piano.

I cannot imagine a more perfect way to celebrate a life in which two people tried their best to live up to their wedding vows. I'm sure that Fern suffered many moments of loneliness and unhappiness during our years together. I had to be away from home months at a time, and she had the burden of raising the children alone. In turn, I suffered great longing for my family as I traveled out on the road. We had our problems and difficult days, as most married couples do. But I'm quite sure it never occurred to either one of us to even think about a divorce. We had married for life, in the eyes of God, and the sacrament of our marriage gave us a strength that kept us close and made our marriage stronger year by year. I would say Fern and I are closer now than ever before. Our children are raised, our grandchildren are a delight, many of the pressures that caused us unhappiness have long since disappeared, and we now share a close and warm companionship studded with wonderful memories which could belong to nobody else but us. It is a rich, wonderful heritage to share.

Once we were re-wed, so to speak, everyone at the party began talking at once, beaming, laughing, exchanging hugs and kisses. Fern and I gave each other engraved anniversary gifts—no, I'm not going to tell you what they were, I have to have *some* secrets! But I will tell you that the children presented us with a lovely montage, a framed collection of pictures Larry had gathered together of some of the high spots of our life—including our original wedding certificate from Sacred Heart Cathedral decorated with a faint tracery of flowers and delicate handwriting stating that Fern Veronica Renner had been wed to Lawrence Welk. At the bottom of the frame was a small engraved brass plaque which read: "Your fifty years together have enriched all our lives with love and devotion. (from) Your grateful family." Do you wonder that I was in tears that afternoon?

But not for long, because over the hubbub Shirley announced that there would now be champagne and hors d'oeuvres for everyone, and it may give you some idea of what high livers the Welks are by the fact that with eighteen people at the party, only two bottles of champagne were consumed, as against countless bottles of sparkling cider! Our daughters had arranged a beautifully decorated dining table centered with iris, yellow tulips, peach-colored roses, and white ranunculus. At least that's what Shirley said—I would have just said there were some pretty pink, white, and purple flowers! We had a gorgeous dinner and a beautiful wedding cake and more sparkling cider and many, many laughs as we "remembered when." As a family I would say we have a pretty good sense of humor. At least there was a great deal of laughter in the room.

Next day, Easter Sunday, was almost a continuation of our celebration. Young "Buns" was serving his very first mass at six-thirty that morning, in his family church about twenty miles away in the San Fernando Valley, and his own family loyally attended. But the rest of us, on our side of the hill, slept a little later and then went to mass at St. Paul's, where we took up practically an entire pew. Then all of us met again for Easter morning brunch at the Bel Air Country Club.

I sat at the head of a long, long table, and looked at each of my family in turn, and out through the huge cathedral windows of the dining room overlooking

West Los Angeles, and back in time to the small sod house where the family of my youth had celebrated Easter, too. Then, we had sat around a plain wooden table in our kitchen. Now, we were in a vast and lovely dining room. But the feeling of love was the same. My family had given me faith and love as a child. So had Fern's. We had tried to do the same for our children, and I thought again of Father's words: "If there were no Bible and no written word, there would still be faith—as long as we have families."

I have been blessed far beyond most men in the world, far beyond anything I deserve. I've been blessed with the privilege of working in a field I love with all my heart, earning my living by bringing a certain amount of happiness and joy to people who might not otherwise receive it. I have been blessed with the love and support of a truly wonderful wife and fine children. I have been privileged to live into my seventies, and celebrate a Golden Wedding Anniversary, after a lifetime marked by earlier illness and setbacks.

There is no way I can possibly express my gratitude, my sense of humble wonder that all this should have been granted to me. But

I think I realize, now more than ever, the power and beauty of love—especially of love sanctified by God's blessing.

My good friend Lon Varnell once said, "Love isn't love till you give it away." Well, perhaps someone else said it before him, but that's where I heard it first. And St. Francis said, "It is in giving love that we receive it." I have found, all through my long life, that this is indeed true. Those who offer affection and consideration to others almost always receive it in kind.

I have received so much love, so much warmth and affection throughout my life, and I want so much to try and say thanks to the many wonderful people who have given me so much of themselves! My own beloved family, of course, and the members of our Musical Family—not only the ones who are with us today, but all those stretching far back through the years who contributed their time, their talents, and their love. They too have become a part of the fiber of my life, as have you wonderful fans who have been so loyal, so supportive, so generous with your warm regard through all these years. Was ever a man so blessed?

I have tried, throughout this book, to share with you some of the thoughts and philosophies that have helped me over the rough spots, and kept me active and happy. I have mentioned how important friends are for happiness in these years, and a sense of humor, faith in God, and something—and someone—to work for. I hope some of these suggestions may be of value to you and bring you some of the peace, fulfillment, and deep contentment which have come to me in these golden, golden years.

I wish for you peace, good health, a vision for the future, long years ahead. But most of all I wish you love—love that can light your life, lighten your life—and give you a hand to hold as the days go by.

Love is the greatest force in the world. And I know it now more than ever.

Epilogue

On the Mother's Day following our Golden Wedding Anniversary, Fern received a beautiful card from our grandson Jimmy, Donna's eldest son. On it he wrote that he was enclosing a copy of a prayer he had written for our 50th anniversary. "I didn't express all the thoughts in this prayer at the service," he wrote, "and I wanted to write them down for you to let you know how much I love and admire you and Grandpa."

When Fern and I read it, we were deeply touched. It meant so much to us we would like to reproduce it for you now, just as it came to us from Jimmy.

Jimmy's Prayer

Father,

Thank you especially for the incredible spirit that you have given Granny and Grandpa. You have blessed them with vitality, perseverance, and an enthusiasm for life which sparkles in their eyes, and they have used these gifts not just for themselves but to make the lives of other people happier. We remember the way that Granny has dedicated herself to a life of sharing her love and strength with others through nursing and raising a family. And we also remember how Grandpa has devoted his life to sharing with countless people the musical spirit that is within him.

Thank you, Father, for the fifty years of marriage that you have given to these two beautiful people. Thank you for nurturing this common spirit within them and letting it blossom out in so many wonderful ways. Thank you for the song in their hearts and the good it has done in the world, and please bless and keep them always.

The publishers hope that this Large Print Book has brought you pleasurable reading. Each title is designed to make the text as easy to see as possible. G. K. Hall Large Print Books are available from your library and your local bookstore. Or you can receive information on upcoming and current Large Print Books by mail and order directly from the publisher. Just send your name and address to:

G. K. Hall & Co.
70 Lincoln Street
Boston, Mass. 02111

Large print edition designed by
Cindy Schrom.
Composed in 18 pt English Times
on an Editwriter 7700
by Cheryl Yodlin of G.K. Hall Corp.